Made with LOVE & PLANTS

by

Tammy Fry

This book is dedicated to my boys, Josh and Kai, and my husband Rich.
But it is also dedicated to you, the reader, for you were my inspiration for writing this book.

Published in 2021 by
  Penguin Random House South Africa (Pty) Ltd
Company Reg. No. 1953/000441/07
The Estuaries, 4 Oxbow Crescent, Century Avenue,
  Century City, 7441
P O Box 1144, Cape Town 8000, South Africa

ISBN: 978-1-43231-089-9

Reproduction by Studio Repro and Hirt & Carter Cape (Pty) Ltd
Printed and bound in Singapore by 1010 Printing International Ltd

Publisher: Beverley Dodd
Managing editor: Cecilia Barfield
Designer: Randall Watson
Cover Designer: Jose Morte
Photographers: Nigel Deary,
  Sonja Wrethman (lifestyle photographs & cover image)
Stylist: Lisa Clark
Illustrator: Riosha Kuar
Proofreader and indexer: Linda de Villiers

FSC MIX Paper from responsible sources FSC® C016973

READERS, PLEASE NOTE:
The advice, suggestions and recipes in this book are intended as a guide to following a plant-based lifestyle, whether for reasons
of health or ethics. However, this information is not intended to provide medical advice and it should not replace the guidance
of a qualified healthcare professional. Decisions about your or your family's health should be made by you and your healthcare
provider/s, based on the specific circumstances of your or your family's health, risk factors, family history and other considerations.
The author and publishers have made every effort to ensure that the information in this book is safe and accurate, but they
cannot accept liability for any resulting injury, or loss or damage to either property or person, whether direct or consequential and
howsoever arising.

CONTENTS

LIVING

A

PLANT-BASED LIFE

MY STORY

I grew up in South Africa where my first home was humble – basically a shack with four walls, a tin roof, no partitioning walls and no running water. We had to collect water from a nearby river and store it in 25-litre drums.

But I should start at the beginning. I was born to a goat farmer dad and a mum who taught at the local village school. Day after day I saw how goats were sold for slaughter, but I soon realised that if i named the individual goats, they crossed the fine line from being 'units of currency' to beloved pets. So I started naming as many of them as possible. I have an enquiring mind and even as a young girl, I questioned everything: 'A drumstick – you play drums with that – but what IS THIS?' (while staring at a chicken leg). Obviously, I was a born vegetarian and that was that. However, 35 years ago in South Africa vegetarianism was almost an unknown concept. Little did I know the challenges I would face growing up in a country where a meat-eating culture was predominant, and the old belief system prevailed – you had to eat meat to be strong and healthy.

Dad left goat farming and started a construction business after learning the trade from my grandfather, so we moved from the farm and into the city. Life took a new turn, and we became familiar with building sites and seesaws made of wooden planks carefully placed over bags of stones, bricks and sand. Entrepreneurs work hard so play time, family time and work time were all rolled into one!

But one day, everything changed again, forever. Dad walked into the house after taking off his building boots at the door and announced that he too was 'never going to eat meat again!' – this after inspecting his most recent construction project, a 4 000-sow piggery.

We had now become a family of vegetarians, in South Africa. Dinner-table conversation included the trivial school day report-backs as well as discussions on morality, ethics, the state of the world, and an update on the latest plant-based burger recipe that my parents were working on as part of a range of high-protein replacements for meat (an unknown concept 30 years ago), mostly just for our own family and a few friends. When the queue of 'friends' lining up at our gate lengthened and the cooking pot could no longer fit the number of sausages required to fulfil the demand, my parents decided it was time to up the ante and a plant-based business was born. The Fry Family Food Company was established in 1991.

Navigating the world as a vegetarian in a country of meat lovers was tough. At school, I was the only vegetarian among a few hundred students and faced much criticism about my dietary choices. I took up karate and literally fought my way to the top – in 1990 (aged nine) I made the junior national karate team and continued to represent my country for over nine years as a junior and a further ten years as a senior. In my final year at school, I won the Junior World Shotokan Championships. That's when it happened – people started asking questions about my plant-based diet, and 'inspiring change' became my mantra.

Fry's was so much a part of my life, so it made sense that after I completed my studies, I began to help out in the family business. I started the marketing department. Dad relegated me to the pre-weighing warehouse, where I was to 'market' and manage the pre-weighing team. Armed with a mop-cap and laptop, I found myself sitting in the middle of a warehouse, at an upcycled pallet desk covered in spice dust and smelling of burger patties!

I met my husband-to-be, sitting at that very desk. We had so much in common with our heavy sports training schedules, love of the outdoors and bush, as well as a love of the ocean and surfing, but there was one sticking point. He was a no ordinary 'omni' – he was a three-meats and one-veg kind of guy with a strong will to boot. How were two people with such differing viewpoints going to reach a compromise? I wasn't a marketer for nothing so I took this on as a personal challenge to see if I could change him. They say you should never try to change your partner, and there I was, devising a plan to do just that. Thank goodness for Fry's products because I never once cooked meat in the house, but he devoured every meal thinking it was meat. Until I proudly announced that it was, in fact, meat free.

Then came children and a whole new set of challenges. Being a parent means that you have subscribed to, well, everything – sleep deprivation, moments of insanity and confusion, decision making, housekeeping, nursing, teaching, being the world's best hairdresser while sporting a mom-bun and carrying dry shampoo in your handbag, becoming a monster slayer, a yogi master, entrepreneur, and conscious consumer, reading food labels, recycling, meditating and trying to follow an organic, plant-based diet! I can see all the parents out there nodding in agreement.

Keeping it simple was my go-to motto once I became a mother of two very healthy, very active boys.

I have dedicated my life to inspiring people to change to a plant-based diet, staying fit and healthy, marketing a plant-based life and The Fry Family Food Co, speaking to audiences around the world on plant-based advocacy, coaching plant-based nutrition and running workshops on transitioning to a plant-based lifestyle. On *my* journey I have learnt:

• inspire others by your actions and the way you live your life;

• go out there and live your best, happiest and healthiest life;

• honour your mind, body and spirit daily; and,

• as Mother Teresa said, 'Spread love everywhere you go. Let no one come to you without leaving happier.'

I wrote this book to help and guide you through *your* journey to plant-based living. Remember to be kind to yourself and don't expect everything to fall into place overnight. Be less concerned with perfection and embrace the changes with great self-love. Dear reader, I hope it will help you.

MADE WITH LOVE AND PLANTS

TAMMY

X

WHY A PLANT-BASED DIET?

When I consider all the significant moments of my life, I can honestly say that I have several reasons for being plant based. It all started when, as a young girl, I did not want to eat animals because I loved them. An animal was an animal, whether it was a chicken, a dog, a pig, a cow or a llama. And I was not going to eat any of them. Once I started training hard for competitions, health and athletic performance enhanced my reasons. Now, as a mother, I care deeply for the planet and the oceans and hope to leave a better planet for my children.

FOR THE ANIMALS

Simply put, a plant-based diet shows more compassion to animals, and not just companion animals that we give names to, but all animals. We are all born compassionate and yet the way we live is discordant with our innate nature – the result of conditioning whereby our food is determined by habits and culture. Human beings are able to compartmentalise emotions and remove themselves from the devastating reality that exists 'behind closed doors'. In order to raise animals more cost effectively for human consumption, we have seen the rise of factory farming; animals are raised in horrific conditions – cramped spaces and in some cases no space at all, no access to fresh air and exercise, exposed to inhumane practises such as debeaking, fed poor quality, genetically modified grains and legumes, and kept alive by an array of antibiotics. As Leo Tolstoy said: 'If slaughterhouses had glass walls, we would all be vegetarian.'

What about dairy?

Cows, like humans, produce milk when they have calves. We interfere by drinking the milk that cows produce for their offspring. The calf is removed from its mother just 24 hours after being born. These calves are essentially the by-products of dairy production. All male calves and about a quarter of female calves are destined for slaughter to produce veal, leather and animal rennet used in cheese production. The remaining heifer calves become milk-producing cows.

The reason dairy cows produce so much milk is because they're impregnated and fed growth hormones by farmers. Today's dairy cows are artificially inseminated once a year and produce one calf on average per year. They are subjected to mechanised milking for ten months a year, and for seven of those months they are pregnant. They are considered 'productive' for only two years and are slaughtered when their milk production drops.

Turning dairy cows into milk-producing machines has led to ever-increasing rates of mastitis (udder infections), which is the leading cause of dairy cow mortality. This industry has changed dramatically from what it used to be just 50 years ago. Now each cow produces two-and-a-half times more milk than then.

What about eggs?

Egg-laying hens are exposed to terrible suffering. Caged hens are severely confined in small cages for their entire lives – the size of the area in which they have to live is approximately the size of an A4 sheet of paper. Hens can live up to ten years (our family hen, Henrietta, lived to 13!), but in this commercially driven industry their lives cease to have value the day their egg production slows down, at which point they are slaughtered.

Of course, male chicks don't produce eggs, so they have no value to the egg industry. On their first day of life at hatcheries, they are put through grinders or macerators. This is known as chick culling and occurs in all industrialised egg production, including organic, free-range and battery-caged egg production.

FOR THE ENVIRONMENT

By moving to a plant-based diet, we can reduce the impact of climate change, rainforest destruction, and pollution, while saving water and other precious resources. In fact, raising animals for food produces more greenhouse gas emissions than all the cars, planes, and other forms of transportation combined.

WATER RESOURCES: It is well known that 'growing animals for food' is extremely water intensive. For instance, 16 000 litres of water are required to produce 1kg of meat, compared to 200 litres of water for 1kg of bread. If you were to cut out meat for just one day, you would effectively save 5 530 litres of water, which equates to a seven-minute shower every day for 50 days.

LAND RESOURCES: Monoculture crops are very destructive to ecosystems and in most cases, the cause of deforestation; 70% of these crops are fed to livestock. It is estimated that an additional 800 million people could be fed by the grain produced in the US for livestock feed, so land resources could be better used to feed people and contribute to the solution to world hunger.

OCEAN RESOURCES: It has been predicted that, based on current utilisation of the ocean's resources, the ocean's ecosystem faces a full collapse by 2048. The seafood industry is plundering the ocean of life. There are not enough fish in the world's oceans to feed seven billion human beings and another ten billion domestic animals. There are 17 major fishing zones, of which 14 are completely depleted or in serious decline, with just three remaining. We are now fishing down the food chain, catching smaller and smaller fish, a sure sign that the larger predator fish are in short supply. Current fishing systems, including longlining and purse seine nets, are extremely destructive and wasteful. Of every 1 kg of targeted fish caught, there is almost 10 kg of bycatch (unwanted fish that often die in the nets and are thrown back into the ocean). Dragnets used to catch prawns and other 'bottom dwellers' have almost completely destroyed the population of seahorses, which are now on the endangered species list.

Why is it that we stop using plastic straws to save fish, but don't want to stop eating fish to save fish? Cows are now the oceans greatest predator eating more fish (in the form of fish meal) than humans, seals, sharks and dolphins combined.

FOR YOUR HEALTH

The developed world is suffering from many chronic diseases, a good number of which could be prevented through diet and good nutrition. As a result, the interest in holistic health, natural medicine and preventative lifestyle medicine is on the increase.

A report in the *Lancet** states: 'Unhealthy diets pose a greater risk to morbidity and mortality than does unsafe sex, and alcohol, drug and tobacco use combined. Because much of the world's population is inadequately nourished and many environmental systems and processes are pushed beyond safe boundaries by food production, a global transformation of the food system is urgently needed.'

A well-planned and executed plant-based diet is known to have many great health benefits:

It's a great way to feel lighter and more energetic. Plant-based foods are easier to digest than animal-based foods, which means that the food 'feels lighter' in your gut and the digestion process requires less energy and time, leaving you more energetic.

A great way to alkalise your body. In theory a high-acid diet creates a breeding ground for disease and leads to poor health. Some of the symptoms of a low pH or acidity in your system include: aching joints, weight gain, carb and sugar cravings, and brain fog. Test strips are available from most health shops to test your pH. An alkaline diet is the opposite of a typical Western diet as it's based on the idea that optimal health comes from balancing the body's pH by eating more veggies and fruit, as well as legumes, grains and nuts.

'The greatest threat to our planet is the belief that someone else will save it'

ROBERT SWAN

ACID/ALKALINE FOOD CHART

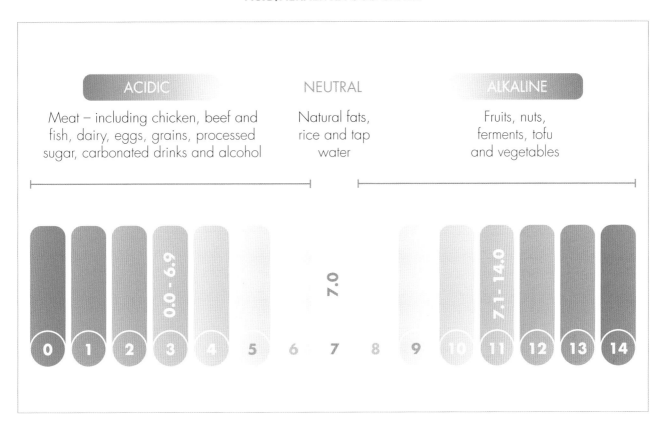

Eat loads of fibre. Plants contain fibre, while meat and dairy do not. By eating a plant-based diet rich in a variety of fruit and vegetables, you will naturally be getting more fibre. And more fibre means a cleaner gut, less constipation and an overall cleaner, less toxic system.

Whole plant-based foods are lower in cholesterol. Plant foods contain no cholesterol, so by cutting out the foods that contribute to your cholesterol levels, you naturally lower those levels.

Lower your blood pressure. By following a plant-based diet you automatically lower your blood pressure due to a higher intake of potassium-rich foods, because potassium helps to lower blood pressure. Nearly all whole grains, legumes, nuts, seeds, and all fruits and vegetables are high in potassium, whereas animal foods contain little to no potassium.

Less toxins, hormones and antibiotics. Current industrialised systems of raising animals means that animals are fed antibiotics (to keep them free of disease) and hormones (to stimulate growth or production of milk and eggs), thereby reducing costs of production. Furthermore, animals eat a diet of grains and fishmeal. The grains are almost always genetically modified and come from heavily sprayed crops. These pesticides and toxins bio-accumulate in the flesh of the animal, which you then consume. Even long-banned pesticides such as DDT have been found in meat and animal by-products. By eliminating animal products, we also reduce our exposure to these chemicals.

Antibiotics have been used in animal feed for over 50 years. Additives such as Tetracycline, Penicillin, Streptomycin and Bactican are some of the more common additives in feed, according to NIH National Library of Medicine, 'The Human Health Implication of the Use of Antimicrobial Agents in Animal Feeds' by H L Dupont and J H Steele (https://www.ncbi.nlm.nih.gov/pubmed/3321681)

Obtaining nutrients from plant foods allows more room in your diet for health-promoting options. If you make smart choices, a vegan diet can be a really healthy way of eating.

PLANT BASED FOR HUMANITY, WORLD HUNGER AND SUSTAINABILITY

The *Lancet* report*, which was compiled by a group of 30 scientists from around the world states: 'Transformation to healthy diets by 2050 will require substantial dietary shifts. Global consumption of fruits, vegetables, nuts and legumes will have to double, and consumption of foods such as red meat and sugar will have to be reduced by more than 50%. A diet rich in plant-based foods and with fewer animal source foods confers both improved health and environmental benefits.' It also suggests that this shift will help to feed a growing world population, sustainably.

Recommended Resources and Reading:

*The *Lancet* report: 'Food in the Anthropocene: The EAT-Lancet Commission on Healthy Diets From Sustainable Food Systems': Willet, W.; Rockström, Loken, B.J.; Springmann, M.; Lang, T.; Vermeulen, S.; et al; January 2019

Heart Disease: *Prevent and reverse Heart Disease* by Caldwell B. Esselstyn, Jr., M.D.

Cancer: The World Health Organization (WHO)'s International Agency for Research on Cancer (IARC) Monograph (Volume 114, October 2015) classifying processed meat as a Group 1 Carcinogen

The China Study: Campbell, T.C.; Campbell, T.M.; BenBella Books, 2004 – Dr Colin Campbell

General Health: Nutrition Facts with Dr Michael Greger: NutrionFacts.org

'Somewhere inside all of us
is the power to change the world'

Roald Dahl

TRANSITIONING TO
A PLANT-BASED DIET

Going plant based is not always as simple as it may seem. Once you remove the foods that you have habitually eaten your whole life and the excitement of your commitment to make the change wears off, you may find yourself struggling with meal preparation ideas and your nutritional intake. Before you know it, you then find yourself going back to your old habits. New habits are hard to form, and a dietary change is tough for most. I hope the following tips will see you through the process.

DON'T GO COLD TURKEY

If you don't have the support of a nutrition coach or dietician, take your time and see this as a journey. It takes time to learn new recipes, to experiment with new foods, and to adapt to a different way of cooking meals. A really helpful way to start is to go almost-vegan or weekday vegan; this way you may find that you transition naturally and one day realise that you no longer use animal products at all. Not everyone has a 'veganniversary'!

DON'T BE A CARBO-VORE

Pasta, bread and potato chips are not the only vegan foods around. Make sure you are eating a variety of fruits, vegetables, nuts, seeds and grains. Variety is the key and will ensure that you are getting all the macro and micro nutrients that your body needs to function, and will help you to feel energetic and sustained.

PLAN AHEAD

The key to really enjoying a plant-based lifestyle is to plan your meals ahead of time. Not only will you need to factor in extra time at the supermarket to read all the labels, but you must ensure that every meal is delicious so that you don't panic-buy frozen chips at the petrol station store. I know, however, that real life sometimes gets in the way, which is why convenient, tasty, grab-and-go plant-based products are an important addition to your shopping list. They are essential for busy lifestyles.

INSPIRE YOURSELF DAILY

This book may be a source of recipe inspiration for you, but keep inspiring yourself by following plant-based bloggers, buy a few simple pieces of new kitchen equipment and find friends who share your new passion.

STAY IN TOUCH WITH YOUR 'WHY'

You may find that going plant based is much easier than you expected, however there may come a time, whether a week, a month, or a year into your new lifestyle, when you could hit a wall. If this happens, just remind yourself why you made the decision in the first place and the benefits you've felt since making the choice. Watching informative videos about veganism, connecting with plant-based influencers or finding your nearest animal sanctuary, are all ways to remind yourself why you chose this path.

The 'why' needs to be your driver for change. Why are you doing this? Put it up on your fridge. Watching documentaries can really keep you on your path and renew your resolve. Make sure you watch 'What the Health', 'Forks Over Knives', 'Cowspiracy', 'Meet your Meat', 'Earthlings', 'Eating Animals', 'The Game Changers' and 'Dominion'.

THERE IS NO NEED TO FEEL DEPRIVED

Many meat-eaters have a preconception that vegans are restricted to a life of salad and uninspiring bowls of vegetables, when that's simply not the case. Opting for a plant-based diet does not mean you need to sacrifice the things you loved before. From burgers and sausages, ice cream and pies – there are some brilliant alternatives on the market that will make you wonder why you ever ate meat in the first place. Use these plant-based meats and milks to help you with your transition – meat and dairy alternatives taste great – and you can still make all your old favourites and the change won't seem so difficult. Furthermore, these foods are often fortified, so you won't become deficient in critical nutrients.

LET SOMEONE ELSE COOK FOR YOU FROM TIME TO TIME

Look for good vegan restaurants – and support them when you are in need of something different. Game changer!

FIND YOUR TRIBE

I am not saying that once you are a vegan, you need to socialise only with vegans, but find people that are also considering changing or convince your friends to join you. Having a community by your side supporting you can be incredibly comforting. Just knowing that others are on this journey with you makes it that much easier. There is a huge vegan and vegetarian community online offering support, tips and recipe ideas, so you're never too far away from a like-minded individual sharing their plant-based experience.

BE HEALTHY

Veganism doesn't always equal healthy, so it's important to make sure you're eating a varied diet to incorporate all the vitamins and nutrients you need to thrive. See the chapter on meal planning (page 16) and the plant-based food pyramid. You are doing the right thing. Back yourself. And go for it!

GET CREATIVE

Veg-based meals can be exciting, delicious and full of flavour, so take this opportunity to try new foods and experiment with ingredients. There are thousands of recipes online with inspiration and ideas to help you cook amazing new dishes and interesting variations of your old favourites.

HEALTHY EATING ON
A PLANT-BASED DIET

While you probably grew up learning about the traditional food pyramid, you may be less familiar with any of the plant-based versions. In the past, we were taught that animal products play a vital role in our diet, so when switching to a plant-based diet, many people make the assumption that you may lack certain nutrients. This chapter aims to debunk those myths and teach you how to get all the nutrients, in the right balance in a simple pyramid diagram.

So, if you are under the impression that a plant-based diet is complex to follow or that you may end up malnourished, the next few paragraphs should change your mind.

In 2009, the American Dietetic Association published a position paper on vegetarian diets, 'Position of the American Dietitic Association: Vegetarian Diets' in the *Journal of the Academy of Nutrition and Dietetics*, 2009; 109 (7): 1266-1282 (web access: https://jandonline.org/article/S0002-8223(09)00700-7/fulltext). It stated: *'Appropriately planned vegetarian diets, including total vegetarian or vegan diets, are healthful, nutritionally adequate, and may provide health benefits in the prevention and treatment of certain diseases. Well-planned vegetarian diets are appropriate for individuals during all stages of the life cycle, including pregnancy, lactation, infancy, childhood and adolescence, and for athletes.'*

It went on to say: *'The results of an evidence-based review showed that a vegetarian diet is associated with a lower risk of death from ischemic heart disease. Vegetarians also appear to have lower low-density lipoprotein cholesterol levels, lower blood pressure, and lower rates of hypertension and type 2 diabetes than non-vegetarians. Furthermore, vegetarians tend to have a lower body mass index and lower overall cancer rates. Features of a vegetarian diet that may reduce risk of chronic disease include lower intakes of saturated fat and cholesterol and higher intakes of fruits, vegetables, whole grains, nuts, soy products, fibre, and phytochemicals.'*

And now, nearly all major health organisations agree that a diet rich in whole, plant-based foods, whole grains and legumes is beneficial to your health. So, how exactly should you divide up your plate to ensure you are getting the balance right?

THE PLANT-BASED FOOD PYRAMID
This is intended as a guide only. I recommend that you consult a dietician or nutritionist to assist you in developing a personalised plan, depending on your current nutritional requirements.

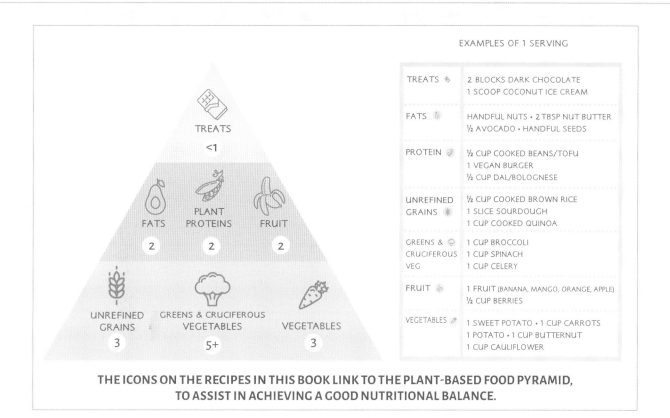

EXAMPLES OF 1 SERVING

TREATS	2 BLOCKS DARK CHOCOLATE 1 SCOOP COCONUT ICE CREAM
FATS	HANDFUL NUTS • 2 TBSP NUT BUTTER ½ AVOCADO • HANDFUL SEEDS
PROTEIN	½ CUP COOKED BEANS/TOFU 1 VEGAN BURGER ½ CUP DAL/BOLOGNESE
UNREFINED GRAINS	½ CUP COOKED BROWN RICE 1 SLICE SOURDOUGH 1 CUP COOKED QUINOA
GREENS & CRUCIFEROUS VEG	1 CUP BROCCOLI 1 CUP SPINACH 1 CUP CELERY
FRUIT	1 FRUIT (BANANA, MANGO, ORANGE, APPLE) ½ CUP BERRIES
VEGETABLES	1 SWEET POTATO • 1 CUP CARROTS 1 POTATO • 1 CUP BUTTERNUT 1 CUP CAULIFLOWER

THE ICONS ON THE RECIPES IN THIS BOOK LINK TO THE PLANT-BASED FOOD PYRAMID, TO ASSIST IN ACHIEVING A GOOD NUTRITIONAL BALANCE.

THE BASE OF THE PYRAMID

This is focused on unrefined grains and vegetables. This is where the bulk of your food, and therefore kilojoules, should come from. Remember to 'eat the rainbow' with as much variety as possible. You should aim for a minimum of five servings of greens (there is no upper limit), three servings of vegetables and three servings of grains a day.

Example (1 day): 1 cup broccoli, 2 cups spinach, 1 cup celery, 1 cup cucumber, 1 slice sourdough bread, 1 cup cooked quinoa, 1 cup cooked brown rice, 1 sweet potato, 1 cup cauliflower, 1 cup carrots, 1 potato, 1 cup butternut.

THE SECOND LEVEL OF THE PYRAMID

This area includes fats, fruits and plant proteins. Fat examples include nuts, seeds, avocado, tahini and cold pressed vegetable oils. Use these in moderation. Fruit examples include berries, papaya, bananas, apples, oranges, watermelon or mangoes. Proteins include foods such as tofu, tempeh, soymilk, legumes, plant-based meats and plant protein powders.

Example (1 day): ½ avocado, 2 tablespoons nut butter, 1 banana, 1 mango, 1 vegan burger, 1 cup cooked beans.

THE TIP OF THE PYRAMID

This includes foods that you should eat occasionally, i.e. the treats! These are processed foods, homemade treats and dark vegan chocolate.

HOW TO GET ALL YOU NEED IN ONE DAY AND A BASIC GUIDE TO MEAL PLANNING

Each recipe in this book has a simple guide to make it easier for you to understand how to build your own daily meal plans, using the principles of the plant-based food pyramid.

EXAMPLES OF MEAL PLANS:

	BREAKFAST	LUNCH	DINNER	SNACKS	TOTAL SERVES	
MONDAY	• Holistic Health Smoothie, p.49 • Handful Vegan Granola, p.52	• Red Pepper and Black Bean Chilli, p.132 • Homemade Corn Tortilla, p.80 or Slice Sourdough	• Cashew Fried Rice with Tofu, p.97	• Handful Raw Nuts and Seeds • Pressed Green Veg Juice	3 grains 2 fruit 5 green	2 veg 2 protein 2 fat
TUESDAY	• Overnight Oats, p.60	• Leftover Cashew Fried Rice with Tofu, p.97	• Red Pepper and Black Bean Chilli, p.132 • Guacamole, p.77	• Fruit • Pressed Green Veg Juice	2 grains 2 fruit 4 green	2 veg 2 protein 2 fat
WEDNESDAY	• Vegan Granola, p.52 • ½ cup Almond Nut Milk, p.157 • Pressed Green Veg Juice	• Coconut Red Lentil Dal, p.135 • Wilted Spinach	• Roasted Cauliflower Biryani, p.94	• Veg Sticks and Hummus	2 grains 5 green	4 veg 2 protein 2 fat
THURSDAY	• Overnight Oats, p.60	• Tofu or Tempeh	• Baby Marrow Fritters, p.82 • Green Salad	• Fruit	3 grains 2 fruit 3 green	2 veg 1 protein 3 fat
FRIDAY	• Calcium Boost Bowl, p.55 • Handful Vegan Granola, p.52	• Unearthed Mexican Sweet Potatoes, p.98 • Roast Sweet Potatoes and fill with Red Pepper and Black Bean Chilli, p.132	• Massaman Thai Curry, p.107	• Cucumber and Celery Sticks	2 grains 3 fruit 3 green	3 veg 3 protein 2 fat
SATURDAY	• Chocolate-chip Protein Pancakes, p.70	• Rice Paper Rolls, p.74	• West African Coconut Curry, p.101 • Quinoa	• Watermelon and Mint	2 grains 2 fruit 2 green 1 treat	3 veg ½ protein 2 fat
SUNDAY	• Tofu Scramble, p.64	• Roasted Butternut, Beetroot and Crispy Sage Tart, p.90	• Leftovers	• 2 Pieces Dark Chocolate	No need to count blocks on a Sunday	

COMMON QUESTIONS AND CHALLENGES
(AND THEIR ANSWERS)

If you already follow a plant-based diet, you may have had these questions from family and friends. And if you are considering adopting a plant-based diet, these will probably answer many of the questions you may have!

WHERE DO YOU GET YOUR PROTEIN FROM?

Your body needs protein to make and repair cells. Protein is essentially a building block for skin, cartilage, blood, muscle and bones.

The USDA recommends 0.8 g protein per 1 kg. The current average intake of protein in developed countries is almost double this. If your kilojoule intake is derived mostly from fruit and vegetables and a wide variety of plant-based foods, rich in all essential amino acids, you will get enough protein. Protein deficiency in the Western World is only really seen in severely malnourished or calorie-deprived patients — a condition known as kwashiorkor. The most perfect food created specifically for humans is breast milk which contains 6% protein — this is enough to double the size of a human baby.

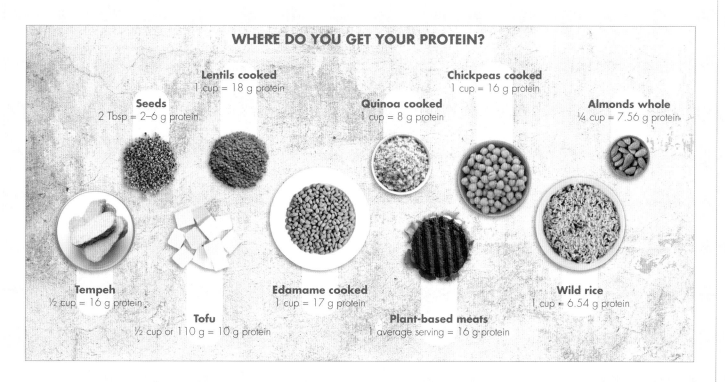

WHERE DO YOU GET YOUR PROTEIN?

Lentils cooked
1 cup = 18 g protein

Chickpeas cooked
1 cup = 16 g protein

Seeds
2 Tbsp = 2–6 g protein

Quinoa cooked
1 cup = 8 g protein

Almonds whole
¼ cup = 7.56 g protein

Tempeh
½ cup = 16 g protein

Edamame cooked
1 cup = 17 g protein

Wild rice
1 cup = 6.54 g protein

Tofu
½ cup or 110 g = 10 g protein

Plant-based meats
1 average serving = 16 g protein

WHERE DO YOU GET YOUR CALCIUM? I THOUGHT CALCIUM IS ONLY FOUND IN DAIRY PRODUCTS

Calcium is needed to build and protect our bones.

Plant-based calcium sources include: spices, basil, soybeans and other beans, nuts, tofu, greens, seaweed, figs, sun-dried tomatoes, peanut butter, almonds, tahini. Buy plant-based milks that are fortified with calcium. Ensure an adequate intake of vitamin D as this increases absorption of the calcium.

Dairy products cause the body to become more acidic. If the body becomes acidic, in a system of self-regulation, calcium will leach from bones, resulting in weakened bones. A study of over 60 000 women (age 39–74) and 45 000 men found that too much milk is associated with increased fractures and mortality (*British Medical Journal* 2014, 349:g6205).

NOTE: Weightbearing and strength training also help build stronger bones, which is one more reason why exercise and weight training are crucial for health and wellness.

WHERE DO YOU GET YOUR IRON?

Iron is a component of haemoglobin which is the substance in the red blood cells that carries oxygen from your lungs to the rest of your body.

Some people have a natural prevalence to iron deficiency, regardless of what diet they follow. The daily recommended intake of iron is 8 mg for males and 18 mg for females in their reproductive years.

Heme iron is the type of iron that comes from animal proteins in our diet. Non-heme iron is found in plant-based foods. Non-heme iron sources: bean and legumes, soybeans and kidney beans, bread, broccoli, dates, peas, rice, pasta, spinach, nuts and seeds, dried fruit, kale, asparagus and tahini.

B_{12} IS ONLY FOUND IN ANIMAL PRODUCTS – THAT MEANS WE WERE DESIGNED TO BE OMNIVORES!
FALSE!

B_{12} helps keeps nerves and blood cells healthy.

Vitamin B_{12} is not found in plant-based foods, that is true. And like humans, animals do not produce B_{12} either. However, it **used** to be found in plant-based foods and soils. So, what is it exactly? We know that it's created by bacteria and fungi that would normally be found on our food and in our water, but due to sterilisation and thorough cleaning followed by manufacturers and producers, the B_{12} is being stripped from the plants. Animals raised for slaughter usually drink dirtier water and foods with high levels of B_{12}. When you consume these animals, you also consume the B_{12} that they have stored in their bodies.

Plant-based sources of B_{12} include: B_{12} supplements (usually taken sublingually) and foods fortified with B_{12} (e.g. some plant milks, soy products and cereals). You can also get a B_{12} injection, which is usually recommended if you have issues absorbing this vitamin from your gut, such as people with Crohn's disease or gastrointestinal issues. I personally prefer taking a daily supplement.

The recommended dietary allowance (RDA) for adults is 2.4 mcg per day (pregnant or breastfeeding women need more), but because only 50% of what you take is actually absorbed, make sure you take at least 6 mcg, preferably more.

Then there's the question of which is a better supplement: cyanocobalamin or methylcobalamin? Cyanocobalamin is a synthetic form of vitamin B_{12} that can be converted to the natural forms methylcobalamin and adenosylcobalamin. The body may absorb cyanocobalamin better and it has both forms of cobalamin, while methylcobalamin has a higher retention rate.

DO YOU NEED MORE ZINC IF YOU FOLLOW A PLANT-BASED DIET?

Zinc is required for numerous bodily processes including, but not limited to, growth, healing, gene expression and DNA production, so zinc is a wonderful supplement for overall health.

The bioavailability of zinc can be reduced by inhibitors in nuts, legumes and grains, so you should consume a little extra if you follow a plant-based diet. Eat oats, brown rice, tofu, chickpeas, and a variety of seeds and nuts.

WHY SHOULD PEOPLE WHO FOLLOW A PLANT-BASED DIET EAT MORE SEAWEED?

Iodine, which is found in seaweed, is used in the production of thyroid hormones and is important for our metabolism; deficiency is the leading cause of intellectual and developmental disability.*

Most people are deficient in iodine whether they are vegan or not. **Worldwide about 2 billion people are iodine deficient.**** You can get iodine from iodised salt. It is easy to overdose with iodine supplements, so I strongly recommend consulting a dietician before any kind of supplementation.

OMEGA-3s FROM VEGETABLE SOURCES? I THOUGHT I NEEDED A DAILY FISH OIL SUPPLEMENT?

Omega-3 fatty acids are linked to heart health and brain development, and are critical to good long-term health and wellness.

Fish oil supplements aren't the only source of omega-3s: think flaxseeds, chia seeds, walnuts, hemp seeds and algae (which is available in supplement format). The essential fatty acid alpha-linolenic acid (ALA) comes from plants and is converted to EPA and DHA (both essential omega-3 fatty acids) in the body. The conversion to omega-3 improves when omega-6 consumption is lower, which is why not all fats are created equal! So, lower your omega-6 consumption and increase omega-3 consumption. Aim for 1:1 ratio – once this balance is achieved, you will reduce inflammation.

Remember, when you take in omega-3 from fish, there's the danger of consuming heavy metals such as mercury, so, choose plant-based sources.

*New York Times, 'In Raising the world's IQ, the secret's in the salt'; McNeil, Donald G. Jr (16 December 2006). Retrieved 4 December 2008.

**The Lancet (12 July 2008), 'Iodine deficiency – way to go yet'.
The Lancet: 372 (9633): 88. doi:10.1016/S0140-6736(08)61009-0. PMID 18620930. Retrieved 10 December 2014.

HEALTH MADE SIMPLE
THE EIGHT KEYS

Never before has chronic lifestyle disease debilitated so many people and affected so many families. I am confident that every one of you reading this book, watches a loved one suffering from a chronic disease. Preventive health is the new buzzword taking the world by storm.

Taking charge means taking responsibility, and the need to take action. The keys to health are relatively simple, but not everyone uses them daily. It's all about establishing good habits that become part of your daily routine. I suggest recreating the eight keys as defined below, on a sheet of paper, and pasting it on your fridge. Make sure there are check boxes to tick each day and monitor your own progress.

☐ **FRESH WATER**

Did you know that 95% of people are dehydrated? And all it takes to correct this is to drink more water! Our bodies are 60% water and thus water is crucial for good health. Drinking more water will not only help improve your complexion, but will boost your energy, improve regularity, flush out toxins, improve your pH and, as a bonus, will help you to lose weight. Often dehydration is misinterpreted as hunger, so next time you think you're hungry, try drinking a large glass of filtered water. And if that's a little bland for you, try adding a slice of lemon or cucumber to the glass. Where possible, avoid drinking from plastic bottles.
Prescription: *Adults need eight glasses per day, children and teens six to seven per day and active people (both adults and children) an additional two glasses per day.*

☐ **FRESH AIR**

This is specifically for people who are office bound. Make sure you get outside and breathe fresh air. Choose fans instead of air conditioners. Inhaling air from different environments has been shown to have some great benefits, so go out into different natural biomes and breathe deeply.
Prescription: *As much as possible. No known side effects. Cannot overdose.*

☐ **SUNSHINE**

Sunshine could almost be classified as a vitamin because your body produces vitamin D when exposed to the sun.
Prescription: *Approximately 20 minutes of sunshine on your skin per day – any time before 10am and after 3pm.*

☐ **EXERCISE**

Exercise is crucial for good health and feel-good vibes. If you work out every day, your body produces hormones that make you happier and less anxious, your energy levels increase, and your risk of chronic disease is reduced. I call exercise my happy pill.

First, find something you enjoy doing and then, do it often! Whether it's CrossFit, hiking, running, surfing, barre, Pilates, yoga, pole dancing, rebounding or just playing soccer with your kids … find it, and do it. Exercise should not feel like a punishment, it should feel good and energise you. In my late teens, I was a kilojoule counter and an exercise addict. Everything I ate was recorded in a food journal, and then I would have to exercise to burn off the kilojoules. This was an unhealthy relationship with exercise and food. Exercise should not be something you do when you feel guilty or down about how you look. Love yourself first, then add a dose of exercise.

There is always time for exercise, whether during a lunch break or getting up 30 minutes earlier to do a yoga session in your PJs, or after work as a stress reliever. Any time is an optimal time to move your body. If you find it really tough to motivate yourself to exercise, you may find that making the decision to do it, is the hardest part. Once you start moving and sweating, the endorphins kick in and you will want more. Once you are in tune with your body, you will know how hard to push, when to push and when to put your feet up. Self-love is critical to connecting to your intuition and trusting it enough to follow it.

Prescription: At least 30 to 45 minutes of exercise daily.

WHOLE, CLEAN, PLANT-BASED FOODS

As the old adage goes, you are what you eat. Whole plant-based foods have a high energy vibration, an array of nutritional benefits, are loaded with fibre and create alkalinity in your body.

Prescription: You need to incorporate as many whole, clean plant-based foods into your daily meals as possible.

POSITIVE, HEALTHY RELATIONSHIPS

An 80-year-long Harvard University study suggests that good relationships, rather than money or status, are the key to good health and happiness. It proved that embracing community helps us live longer and be happier. Moai (Japanese word for a group of life-long friends) is an Okinawan 'longevity' tradition in which social support groups are created during childhood and extend through an entire lifespan. The moai will meet once or twice a week to share food, advice, and generally chat, and the members are committed to each other for life. When a member of a moai needs assistance, the other members are there to help.

Prescription: Find your tribe, connect with your family and move past toxic relationships. Spend time with people that uplift and inspire you.

FINDING YOUR PURPOSE

Having a reason for being, a reason for getting up in the morning has shown to bring not only happiness, but improved health and longevity too.

Prescription: Find that thing that you are passionate about and that increases your self-worth. This may need some soul searching, which is always best done in nature and the early hours of the morning.

SLEEP

Sleep is an important biological function of life and not having enough sleep can negatively affect your mood, your decision-making ability and your motivation. Studies have shown that poor sleepers have an increased risk of heart disease and stroke, whereas people who get sufficient sleep are calmer, happier, more alert and energised.

Prescription: Eight hours a night.

THE BLUE ZONES AND LONGEVITY

WHAT WE CAN LEARN FROM PEOPLE WHO BECOME CENTENARIANS?

I am not just talking about *living* to 100, I am talking about people *thriving* until they are 100, and older! It's one thing to reach a great age, kept alive by a concoction of pharmaceutical drugs, and quite another to live a healthy, happy and fulfilled life.

There are pockets of people in the world who live to this age, largely unaffected by cancer, heart disease and diabetes, so why aren't we taking note and learning from the experts, the people themselves? I personally found these studies fascinating and set about trying to recreate many of the identified characteristics and ways of living and eating in my own life.

So, what exactly are the Blue Zones?

American explorer and best-selling author, Dan Buettner, identified five regions that he classified as 'Blue Zones', where longevity has been identified and validated. These areas are Okinawa (Japan), Nicoya (Costa Rica), Icaria (Greece), Sardinia (Italy) and the Seventh-Day Adventists in Loma Linda (California, US). People living in these areas enjoy more years of good health and suffer only a fraction of the diseases that commonly kill people in other more developed parts of the world.

Characteristics of various Blue Zones were identified and recorded. The most common of these characteristics that were shared by the majority of the Blue Zones included constant moderate activity, a sense of community, and following primarily a plant-based diet with the inclusion of legumes, no smoking and spending time with family. Some of the other characteristics shared by more than two of the Blue Zones included empowered women, sunshine, gardening, no time urgency and wholegrains in the diet.

After learning about the Blue Zones and their characteristics, my husband and I decided that we needed to make some changes in our own lives. We decided to relocate and break our nine-to-five cycle of work, sitting at a computer, all day, every day. It would require a change in the way we ate, the way we spent our time as a family, and some of our priorities in life.

We pledged to work less structured hours, break some of our bad habits, connect meaningfully with nature and with people who inspired us and made us happy. Family would come first, we would go on adventures and spend more time together and less time on 'technology'. We would do whatever it was that made us insanely happy. And of course, we would eat more legumes! Was it easy to take these steps? NO. Was it worth it? Absolutely.

Change, of course, can be distressing for some, and especially for me. The first two years were definitely challenging, and we had to keep coming back to our 'why', and our motivation. What do we love about the changes we have made? Our life is simpler, happier and healthier. We are more connected to our children.

We have less financial wealth, but bucket loads of fulfillment. Our gratitude journals are full, as are our daily journals. No two days are the same and our experiences list is long. Our life now feels like one big adventure and each day is exciting and new. We had to remind ourselves, that growth comes from change.

I had to ask myself these questions over and over again: Is today different from yesterday? Am I growing? If not, am I dying? Is the version of me today the same or similar version of my 20-year-old self? If the answers were yes, I needed to do something about it. I wanted to chase the ultimate version of myself and the Blue Zones gave me that opportunity; to stop talking about it and start chasing it.

'The secret to living well and longer is to eat half, walk double, laugh triple and love without measure.'
Tibetan Proverb

CONSCIOUS EATING
MAKING YOU HAPPIER ONE BITE AT A TIME!

WHAT IS CONSCIOUS EATING AND HOW TO PRACTISE IT

One of the greatest journeys you can embark on, is the journey to find your happy place when it comes to your mind, body and spirit. The place where the foods you eat make you feel nourished, light, and give you energy; where you feel a connection to the food and an ultimate sense of wellbeing. Conscious eating is the deliberate and intentional consumption of foods, being absolutely aware of the impact that these foods have on the environment, the people involved in the production of them, how they're packaged and the positive or negative effect these foods may have on your own health.

Making more conscious choices means that you are choosing foods with a lower environmental impact made by people who are treated fairly in the workplace, intentionally avoiding foods that come from animals and trying to obtain locally-grown, chemical-free produce. Eat and live consciously.

SOME IDEAS TO EAT MORE CONSCIOUSLY

☐ **Start your day right**

Hot water and a squeeze of lemon.

The steps you take at the start of a day often determine the outcomes of that day. By making a conscious choice when you wake up, you are setting yourself up for success. Hot water and lemon will not only alkalise your body, but will also help promote the secretion of stomach acids before you eat your first meal of the day.

Make sure you drink at least eight glasses of water during the day. Thirst is often misinterpreted as hunger and so we reach for food when in fact we are just thirsty. Stay hydrated and you will feel less hungry throughout the day. Drinking water just before or just after eating dilutes stomach acids that make digestion slower and less efficient, so try to drink the water between mealtimes.

☐ **Eat when you are hungry and stop when you are full**

Intermittent fasting can indicate when you are actually hungry.

Hunger is beneficial to developing a healthy relationship with food. It is difficult in today's world where food is available everywhere you go: retail stores, restaurants, petrol stations and fast food outlets all sell a plethora of foods and drinks designed to keep you coming back for more. This is where willpower and planning are crucial – both easily learned skills. We often eat when we aren't hungry – boredom, stress, thirst, emotions and social occasions, all of which wreak havoc with our food consumption. Never expose yourself to temptation when you are hungry, so keep some healthy snacks in your bag or car for moments like these.

☐ **Dinner table sanctuary**

For busy families this can be a challenge, but eating around a table is really important for conscious eating.

Connecting with your family, friends and fur family is vital to generating the positive emotions you need to feel while eating. Try making your dinner table a tech-free zone – no TV, no phones, no headphones. Eliminate distractions. If it can't be done every day, set aside certain times where it is mandatory for the family to eat together around a table.

☐ Consider where your food comes from

Supermarkets have disconnected us from the biome and source of our food, with little resemblance to what it is made of. Buy from ethical companies and make sure you research the company values too. If possible, buy local, organic produce and venture into nature to breathe in the air of the biome where this food is grown. This will build your gut bacteria, which in turn will better digest the food and build an almost 'spiritual connection' with the food you consume. Feeling connected to the brand or the food will enhance your gratitude for the hands that grew, harvested and prepared it.

☐ How your food is packaged

It would be almost impossible to buy foods with no packaging at all, especially if you have a family. However, if we all make an effort to reduce the number of garbage bags we send to the landfill each week, we can make a difference. Try composting at home or purchasing a simple worm farm for all your compostable waste.

☐ Consider your gut

Your gut is the one barrier you have between the outside world and your body. If you damage the gut, you damage the barrier and trigger many health problems. Following closely is your immune system. Once your gut is damaged, it allows toxins and pesticides from food to pass through, and your immune system will kick into overdrive to protect you and remove the harmful substances. Hello gluten intolerance, food allergies, hypersensitivities and eventually chronic lifestyle disease as the immune system is constantly overwhelmed and unable to do the job it was designed to do.

☐ Practise self love

The more you love and accept yourself, the less likely you are to binge on unhealthy foods. Treat your body as a temple and your food choices will start to align with your belief system. If you fall off the wagon from time to time, don't stress, your body is clever enough to burn more kilojoules and reduce your appetite the next day. It is designed to regulate your weight, by adjusting your appetite and hormones; you just need to trust and listen to it!

POINTS TO REMEMBER

Implementing one or two of these ideas will start you on your journey to a greater level of consciousness and awareness. You might just catch yourself smiling a little bit more too!

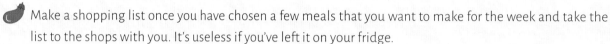

NAVIGATING THE SUPERMARKET
AND DECODING LABELS

Shopping can be a daunting task, especially when embracing a new way of eating and changing old habits. With thousands of products from which to choose, here are a few ideas to keep you on the right health track.

- Make a shopping list once you have chosen a few meals that you want to make for the week and take the list to the shops with you. It's useless if you've left it on your fridge.
- Usually, the less processed foods are found on the perimeter of the supermarket, such as vegetables and fruit, and refrigerated and frozen wholefoods. Remember that a product found in the chiller usually has a 20–40-day shelf life (a requirement of most supermarkets), which means that the food usually has quite a nasty list of preservatives.
- Don't be scared of the freezer section of the supermarket or your freezer at home. Foods found in the freezer in the supermarket very rarely contain preservatives. Use your home freezer for leftovers, homemade breads, chopped herbs, chopped chillies, homemade dips, smoothie bananas, etc. If you aren't sure if something is safe to freeze, search online for information.
- Shop around. Sometimes the best place to buy veggies may not be the best place to buy dry or frozen foods, so make sure you do your homework when it comes to price, quality and trustworthiness.
- Shopping online has transformed the way we can purchase our food. You can order organic and locally produced fruit and vegetables from reputable small businesses and have them delivered to your door. Nearly every major retailer offers online shopping and you can often choose your hours of delivery – no more last-minute, crazy shopping to buy dinner.
- Don't always trust claims on packaging. Familiarise yourself with food labels and how to read them with some understanding. Thereafter make your own, informed choice (see the guidelines below).
- Herbs and spices not only add flavour to your meals, but can often boost the nutritional content of a meal. If you can buy them in bulk, it's possible to avoid excess packaging and costs.
- Never forget the golden rule: do not shop when you are hungry. Avoid pre-prepared meals and convenience meals; they're often expensive and have very small portion sizes.

A GUIDE TO READING NUTRITION LABELS
Once you understand labels, it will become easier to read them. Find what you are looking for and start choosing brands you trust (not just the ones with a great looking package!). It's so worth taking the time to read a label and you will thank yourself in the long run.

NUTRITIONAL INFORMATION

Servings per pack: 4   Serving size 20 g

	Average per serve	Average per 100 g
Energy	100 cal (420 kJ)	500 cal (2100 kJ)
Protein	3 g	15 g
Fat — total	2.5 g	12.5 g
Saturated	0.5 g	2.5 g
Carbohydrate	10 g	50 g
Sugars	1 g	5 g
Sodium	4 mg	20 mg

Check out the serving size

Look here for both the serving size (the amount of food people typically eat at one time) and the number of servings in the package. Compare this to your portion size (the amount you actually eat).

Total calories or kilojoules

A calorie or kilojoule is a unit that measures energy. Don't be too caught up in the calorie/kilojoule trap – if the ingredients are healthy, then the product is healthy. Focus on the big picture of food intake over a whole day as opposed to one kind of food.

- Average kilojoule requirement for men: 10 000–12 000 kJ per day
- Average kilojoule requirement for women: 8 000–10 000 kJ per day

If you are training or working a more strenuous job, you may need more calories/kilojoules.

To lose weight, choose healthy, sustaining whole foods throughout the day. Avoid empty calorie/kilojoule or high-fat snacks, sauces and additional oils, and sugary drinks (including fruit juice).

Check out the sugar content

As a rule of thumb, only buy foods with a sugar content of less than 4–5 g per 100 g (4 g is equal to 1 teaspoon of sugar). Anything more than 5 teaspoons of sugar for an adult and 3 teaspoons for a child per day (not counting sugar found in whole fruit) is too much. The average American eats approximately 17 teaspoons of sugar per day, and according to an article 'Facts about sugar-sweetened beverages (SSBs) and obesity in South Africa' on the University of the Witwatersrand, Johannesburg, research news website from 2016 (www.wits.ac.za/news/latest-news/research-news/2016/2016-04/ssb-tax-home/sugar-facts/), South Africans consume 12–24 teaspoons of sugar per day.

Some examples of foods high in sugar:
- granola/snack bars: average 6–15 g sugar per bar (1.5–4 teaspoons sugar per bar)
- flavoured yoghurt: average 10–14 g per serving
- 1 can carbonated soft drink/energy drink: average 40–50 g sugar
- sauces such as tomato sauce, BBQ sauce and many dressings contain high amounts of sugar, so read the label to check

Why is sugar in fruit different?
Because fruit contains fibre! The body breaks down refined sugar very quickly, causing insulin and blood sugar levels to increase almost immediately. The fibre in fruit slows down the metabolism of the fruit sugars, resulting in a slower release of sugar into the body and a feeling of satiety. The benefits of eating fruit far outweigh the negatives, because fruit also contains phytonutrients, polyphenols, antioxidants, minerals and vitamins.

Check out the fat breakdown
Look for foods with the lowest saturated fat and never buy foods containing trans-fats or hydrogenated fats. Saturated fat and trans-fat are linked to an increased risk of heart disease. Choose foods that contribute zero to cholesterol. Our bodies are cholesterol-conserving machines and we make our own cholesterol, so we do not need a diet of cholesterol-inducing foods.

The VIP guest – fibre
Fibre is perhaps one of the most crucial elements of good health as it performs some critical functions:
- helps build the gut biome (especially prebiotic fibre)
- improves bowel movements and stool consistency
- reduces haemorrhoids
- lowers cholesterol
- controls blood sugar levels
- and, is a marker for longevity

So, considering that the symptoms of too little fibre in the diet are constipation, bloated stomach, sugar highs and lows, high cholesterol, a feeling of constant hunger and carrying extra body weight, I would say people on a traditional Western diet are deficient in fibre.

How much fibre do you actually need?

The United States Department of Agriculture (USDA), which provides science-based advice on matters of medicine and health, recommends the following daily fibre for adults under 50: 38 g for men and 25 g for women and for over 50s: 30 g for men and 21 g for women.

THE INGREDIENTS LIST

Foods with more than one ingredient must have an ingredient list on the label, listed in descending order by weight, so pay attention to the first few ingredients. What to look out for:

Hidden sugars

To identify hidden sugars, look for these words:

- syrup (e.g. corn syrup)
- the ingredient ends in 'ose' (e.g. fructose, dextrose, sucrose)
- 'sugar' is in the name (e.g. brown sugar, cane sugar)
- concentrates (e.g. juice concentrate)

Artificial sweeteners

Avoid aspartame, acesulfame-K, sucralose and saccharin. Stevia and monk fruit are acceptable.

E numbers

Not all E numbers are equal and not all scientific or chemical-sounding ingredients are 'bad' for you. There are over 300 food additives and some of these are actually quite healthy. Many of these E numbers originate from natural foods, so in eating a wholefood diet you would be consuming additives anyway. Some examples of healthy E numbers include: E 300 (vitamin C), E 100 (curcumin, also known as turmeric), E 164 (saffron), E 140 (chlorophyll, from green plants), and E 948 (oxygen).

James Kennedy, a high school chemistry teacher in Melbourne, Australia, compiled ingredient lists for various natural foods. His analysis of an ordinary banana has become particularly popular, which you can find on the internet.

Health claims

Don't be too sold on health claims on packaging. Once you know how to read labels, you will make better choices, and not be influenced by marketing propaganda.

'We do not inherit
the earth from our forefathers,
we borrow it from our children.'
Native American Proverb

VEGAN PARENTING 101

Here's the thing ... there is no such thing as a perfect parent. So remember to give yourself a break sometimes. Try not to set yourself up for failure by having too high expectations and thinking that perfection is attainable. Keep the bigger picture in mind – if things don't quite go to plan, don't beat yourself up about it.

I'm often asked if children are able to derive sufficient protein on a plant-based diet, which is understandable given the importance of protein for a growing body. The recommended protein intake for a child is 1 g for every 1 kg of bodyweight and according to the National Academies of Sciences, Engineering and Medicine, 10–30% of a person's total energy intake should come from protein. A diet encompassing a wide variety of plant-based foods, including beans, legumes, nuts, broccoli and whole grains, will provide sufficient protein.

Soy protein provides the same quality of protein as meat and contains all essential amino acids. Other common nutritional concerns about raising children on a plant-based diet are usually centred around iron and omega-3 fatty acids. Non-heme iron is found in a variety of plant-based foods such as leafy greens, beans and grains, and nuts and seeds. Omega-3 can easily be replicated in a plant-based diet with flaxseeds, hemp seeds and chia seeds, to name just a few. Plant-based foods are higher in a wide variety of vitamins and minerals, contain fibre and have far less sodium, saturated fats and cholesterol than their meat- and dairy-based counterparts, not to mention the prevalence of antibiotics and other scary pharmaceuticals commonly found in meat and dairy products.

With the increasing awareness of the benefits of plant-based eating, there are more and more child-friendly plant-based options on the market. It is so much easier these days to replicate foods that kids will eat and enjoy in plant-based versions, rather than forcing them to eat a plate of wilted spinach.

In raising my own boys, I have never found it difficult to explain to them why we eat plant based, and they are completely on board with the decisions we make as a family. I have always shared with them the truth about where our food comes from (without scaring them). Despite our choices as a family they never feel left out – they still enjoy sausage rolls, burgers and pizzas occasionally, just the vegan versions! When they are out with friends, I allow them to make their own choices about what to eat. It can be tough for children to navigate a birthday party with non-vegan cakes, treats and sweets, so in these instances I try my best to guide them.

Being a parent presents many serious challenges, but bringing up vegan children in a non-vegan world – yes, you need a superhero outfit to cope with that. It's tough, really tough. And I sympathise. So, here are a few ideas to help you out and encourage your children (and possibly partner too) to eat more plants. These are purely from my personal experience as a parent, so let's support one another through this navigational minefield!

- Remember, your children are not you. It is up to you to teach them the values that you hold as a family unit. You are there to guide them and inspire them. If they make different choices as they get older, don't take it personally or as a sign that you have failed.
- Make mealtimes exciting. Be creative in the kitchen with your children — try making food art with the vegetables (think rainbow wraps, noughts and crosses) and become a master of disguise (hide the veggies they don't usually like to eat). Remember to keep it simple though — you want them to see the job through — so something that takes a few minutes to prepare rather than something complicated and time consuming, will make the task more enjoyable.
- Tell stories. My kids grew up calling broccoli 'fairy trees' and beans 'Jack and the Beanstalk'. Make vegetables part of a fun, fantasy world.
- Place a simple salad or veggie sticks onto the table a few minutes before dinner. You might just find your kids snacking on the carrots, sugar peas and cucumbers while you finish preparing dinner.
- Talk about the food you have made. Teach your children about the health benefits (educating yourself and your children will greatly benefit you all), the way you prepared it, and where it comes from (for example, if it's homegrown, from a farm nearby). Talking about where animal products come from too, may help the rest of the family understand your point of view (keep emotions out of these discussions). Be frank, honest and logical.
- Realise that everyone is on their own journey. You can't force your feelings on others. Listen to their point of view, be kind, and give your own thoughts in a non-confrontational way. Plant seeds. Do not judge. Be compassionate.
- Be prepared for events. School events, fundraisers, get-togethers, and kids' parties all typically include animal products. Pack some options for your kids. I always take plant-based sausages or sausage rolls so that my children don't feel 'deprived'.
- Try to grow a few of your own vegetables. If your children have had a hand in growing it, they are more likely to eat it. You don't need a big garden, just a small area where you can grow herbs, or cherry tomatoes or even a dwarf fruit tree. The time taken to grow the food and the caring and watering of it, will help children to develop a conscious connection to the food.
- Be a good role model. If you are sneaking treats from the treat cupboard, they are likely to follow in your footsteps. No pressure!
- Connect with animals. Go to a farm sanctuary together and spend time with rescued animals. Ensure that your children are able to develop real connections with animals.
- Pack a picnic — eating outdoors is not only fun, but may inspire your children to try new foods in a new environment. It's healthy too; when you eat outside, you expose yourself to new bacteria that develop your gut biome. Sit on the grass, put your feet on the ground or lie on your back and feel the earth beneath you.
- Head out to a farmer's market and start teaching your children about seasonal vegetables. Mother Earth knows what you need and when you need it. Nature never ceases to amaze me.

MUST-HAVE
KITCHEN EQUIPMENT

There are an overwhelming number of 'nice-to-haves' that promise to save you time and effort in the kitchen. I'm sure you have bought a few gadgets for your kitchen over time that are gathering dust. This list is short, sweet and functional and will save you money in the long run.

- [ ] Food processor (with a powerful motor): I use a Ninja food processor.

- [ ] A high-speed blender – for blending soups, smoothies, making cashew cheese and nut milks: I have a Ninja blender.

- [ ] A juicer – a lower speed, cold press extraction system is the best for getting the most nutrient value out of your fruit and vegetables.

- [ ] An airfryer – it is great for quick cooking without using oil: I use a Philips airfryer.

- [ ] A good-quality, non-toxic, non-stick pan.

- [ ] A family-size casserole – I prefer the Le Creuset options, which are enamelled cast iron and come with a lifetime warranty.

- [ ] A coffee machine – every family needs one of these.

HEALTHY AND PLANT BASED
ON A BUDGET

A common misconception about healthy, organic, plant-based food, or eating clean, is that it can be expensive.

When my husband resigned his job to start his own business, our budget was tight, and we had to make some personal budget cuts. Yet, we managed to halve our food budget! And we did it without sacrificing our health. Of course, we could have loaded up on bread and peanut butter, noodles and chips, but our goal was to still cook well-balanced and nutritious meals without overspending.

If your goal is to be healthy and happy without breaking the bank each month, these are my own tried and tested suggestions:

GO PLANT BASED

With the World Health Organisation declaring processed meat a Group 1 carcinogen (Tobacco smoking and asbestos are also group 1 carcinogens), consuming meat may result in high medical bills down the line. According to a study published in *The Permanente Journal* in 2015, 'A plant-based diet, atherogenesis, and coronary artery disease prevention' (https://www.ncbi.nlm.nih.gov/pmc/articles/PMC4315380/), following a plant-based diet may be a simple, low-cost intervention to prevent heart disease.

BUY IN BULK

If you don't want to eat the same thing every day – I know I like to switch things up – I suggest purchasing three different packs of 'bulk bases', which you can rotate over a few weeks and which can form the base of your meals. Find your nearest bulk food store or the bulk food section at your supermarket for cheaper bags of beans, pasta, flours and grains such as rice, oats, barley and couscous. Also look for starchy root vegetables, like potatoes and sweet potatoes, which are not only cheap and filling, but also nourishing. Be sure to rotate your bases too so that the nutrition you get varies.

BUY SEASONALLY AND FROZEN

Check out what's in season in your part of the world and create your own planning guide so that you can shop seasonally. It's cheaper and tastier! If possible, visit a farmer's market or buy directly from growers; it's definitely more cost-effective. Additionally, frozen produce can be cheaper than fresh – I know this can't be done with all fruit and veg, but where possible it can make a huge difference. Such fruits and vegetables are flash frozen very soon after they have been harvested and therefore are often more nutritious than fresh produce that's been lying about for days before reaching markets. For an economical meal, I like to make a soup by adding frozen veggies, veg stock, spices and some legumes like lentils (which I sometimes buy dried and then soak and boil them myself).

PLANNING ON A FULL STOMACH

Plan your weekly and snacks meals ahead of time (a bit of a chore on a glorious Sunday afternoon, but well worth the ten minutes of your time). This results in less waste and unnecessary purchases when you're in the supermarket.

SPECIAL OCCASIONS AND DEALS

Plant-based 'meats', like Fry's, obviously don't cost the same as a bag of dried chickpeas, but sometimes you may crave such foods or want something quick and easy to make. Often retailers run special promotions so that you can work them into your budget. When there's a buy-one-get-one-free or bulk pack special, it's a good time to stock up the freezer.

GET COOKING

Cooking from scratch can save you plenty of money, and it doesn't need to take hours of your time if you've planned what you're going to cook. My family and I rarely eat out as I cook all our meals. Eating out should be an occasional treat or something to be avoided altogether if you're on a budget. I prepare meals in large batches (see page 128 Batch Cooks) and freeze the extras and any leftovers. If some produce starts to look a bit worse for wear, I either cook them that day or freeze them immediately.

THOSE PEANUTS AND RED BULL PURCHASES

Convenience stores can wreak havoc with your food budget – ask me, I speak from experience. When Richard and I first got together, we just couldn't seem to save money, so one month we kept the slips from every purchase we had made. We soon identified the problem – peanuts and Red Bull! We now have our own personal budget item called 'peanuts and Red Bull', which is for those last-minute, unexpected, must-have items that we all fall prey to at some point in the month.

GROW WHAT YOU CAN

We may not all have the space to grow our own food, but even with a small verandah or patio and some TLC, you can grow things such as herbs, peppers, radishes, lettuce, kale and vine tomatoes. Start small. It may be an effort initially, but once you get the ball rolling, there is nothing quite like picking your own fresh homegrown produce and including it in the meal of the day!

THE PANTRY

Your pantry (if you're fortunate enough to have one) or food storage cupboard and freezer are the most important spaces in your home – they house the secrets to your and your family's mental and physical health, and ultimately the building blocks to your happiness and longevity.

DRY GOODS PANTRY OR STORAGE AREA
For this the following are essential:
- [ ] An array of glass jars in various sizes
- [ ] Labels for the jars
- [ ] Open shelving

Wherever possible, buy dry goods from bulk foods shops, thereby minimising wasteful packaging and reducing costs. I decant mine into glass jars, label and date-code them. Group like foods together, i.e. flours, grains, legumes, seeds, spices. An organised pantry makes you feel calmer and saves you time when cooking.

A USEFUL STARTER SHOPPING LIST

PANTRY DRY GOODS (Keep those glass jars handy)

Almond meal

Almonds, raw (preferably – better activated)

Bicarbonate of soda – for cleaning and cooking

Black beans

Brown rice

Cashews, raw (preferably – better activated)

Chia seeds

Chickpeas

Coconut milk and coconut cream

Coconut water

Crushed tomato or passata (canned)

Desiccated coconut

Flours (a huge variety available, so choose what you and your body prefer: normal, spelt, chickpea, coconut). You can slowly transition to different flours when you start experimenting with them!

Ground flaxseed

Herbal teas

Lentils (all colours)

LSA (linseed/almond/sunflower) seeds

Maple syrup

Nutritional yeast

Organic oats

Pepitas (a specific variety of pumpkin seeds)

Pitted dates

Psyllium husk

Puffed amaranth

Quinoa (tricolour)

Red kidney beans

Rice malt syrup

Sweetcorn (canned)

Walnuts, raw

FATS AND OILS

Coconut oil – for bathing, skin moisturiser, cooking and baking

Flaxseed oil – add to smoothies, and as salad dressing

Macadamia oil

Natural peanut butter

Olive oil

Tahini

HERBS AND SPICES

Black pepper

Cardamom

Cinnamon

Coriander

Cumin

Garam masala

Garlic

Ginger

Pink Himalayan salt

Rosemary

Smoky paprika

Turmeric

FRESH FRUIT AND VEGETABLES
(Choose seasonal if possible)

Apples

Avocados

Bananas

Beetroot

Berries

Broccoli

Carrots

Coriander

Garlic

Ginger

Green beans

Green salad leaves

Lemons & limes

Onions

Peppers

Red chillies

Snow peas & sugar snaps

Spring onions

Sweet potatoes

Tomatoes

FOR THE FRIDGE AND FREEZER

Coconut yoghurt with live cultures

Frozen fruits

Hummus

Kombucha

Plant-based meats

Plant milk (homemade)

Sauerkraut/kimchi

Tempeh

Tofu

BREAKFAST

HOW TO MAKE A PERFECT SMOOTHIE

- Use frozen fruit, but peel it before freezing, especially bananas. Frozen fruit is a great smoothie thickener.

- Don't mix colours such as purple and green as they will turn brown and unappetising.

- Use good fats like nut butter and frozen avocado for a smooth, creamy flavour and texture. (For weight loss, reduce the fats and fruits and add more greens.)

- Mixing foods: Rule of thumb – never mix dairy and fruit. It is not surprising to see so many digestive aids on the market today. Poor food combinations can cause indigestion, fermentation, and gas formation in the gut and could eventually lead to toxaemia and disease. Rather use coconut milk or coconut water as the base for a smoothie. Almond milk is great for protein smoothies.

- Add frozen baby spinach to increase nutrient intake (it doesn't taste of anything!).

- Smoothies are an awesome way to increase nutrient intake for children, without them knowing the precise contents.

- Add these superfoods: chia seeds (fibre, protein), psyllium husk (fibre), probiotic powder, hemp seeds or hemp protein powder, cacao nibs or powder for energy, maca root powder for energy, pepita seeds (pumpkin seeds) for an array of nutrients (zinc, magnesium, selenium and iron).

- If you want to include a plant-based protein, look for one without added sugar or artificial sweeteners.

- Make a big batch of a smoothie mix and freeze in portions. Frozen smoothies are great for days when you are in a rush and need to grab-and-go; you can enjoy as a frozen smoothie bowl and sprinkle nuts, seed mix or homemade granola on top.

- Always add liquids first, then fruits or vegetables, followed by protein powder and ice.

Add fruit

Banana
Mango
Wild blueberries
Pink pitaya
Strawberries

Choose a liquid

Coconut water
Plant milks

Thicken it

Nut butter
Plant proteins
Oats
Ice cubes
Coconut yoghurt

Up the flavour

Cinnamon
Mint
Maple syrup
Dates
Cacao

Add Superfoods

Pepita seeds   Psyllium husk
Cacao nibs   Turmeric & black pepper
Probiotics   Superfood greens
Flaxseed oil   Hemp seeds
Spinach   Chia seeds
                LSA

THE HIP WIGGLER

1 SERVING

2   1   1

The tastiest smoothie you can make, loaded with the yummiest ingredients around. Find your inner child and go wild!

SERVES: 1 • PREP TIME: 5 min • LEVEL OF DIFFICULTY: 1/5

INGREDIENTS

1 cup almond milk
1 banana, frozen, peeled
   and cut into chunks
½ cup ice cubes
3 dates, pitted
¼ cup raw almonds
¼ cup rolled oats
½ tsp ground cinnamon
¼ tsp vanilla extract
1 Tbsp hemps seeds,
   1 tsp psyllium husk,
   1 Tbsp plant-based
   protein powder,
   1 tsp maca root
   powder (all optional)

Toppings

1 Tbsp shredded coconut
1 tsp cacao nibs
1 Tbsp coconut yoghurt
1 Tbsp crushed
   macadamia nuts

METHOD

Pour the almond milk into the jar of a blender (liquid at the bottom makes it easier to blend). Add all the other ingredients and blend until smooth. Transfer to a jar or glass and sprinkle with your choice of toppings (one, some or all), then devour.

THE GOOD MORNING VIBES SMOOTHIE

1   1   1   1 SERVING

Every parent needs this smoothie in their lives: double shot espresso and anything is possible!

SERVES: 1 • PREP TIME: 5 min • LEVEL OF DIFFICULTY: 1/5

INGREDIENTS

1 cup coconut milk

1 banana, frozen, peeled and cut into chunks

double shot espresso, cooled

1 tsp cacao powder

1 Tbsp cacao nibs

1 Tbsp hemp seeds

2 Tbsp plant-based protein powder

1 tsp maca root powder (optional)

1 tsp psyllium husk (optional)

Toppings

a pinch of espresso grinds

a pinch of cacao powder

METHOD

Pour the coconut milk into the jar of a blender. Add all the other ingredients and blend until smooth. Transfer to a jar or glass and sprinkle over your choice of toppings.

THE RAINBOW UNICORN

3   1   1 SERVING

This smoothie takes a few minutes longer to prepare than a standard smoothie, but your kids will LOVE you for it. It's also pretty and perfect for a summery day.

SERVES: 2 • **PREP TIME:** 8 min • **LEVEL OF DIFFICULTY:** 4/5

LAYER 1
1 banana, frozen, peeled and cut into chunks
½ cup frozen mango chunks
½ cup frozen pink pitaya (dragon fruit)
± ½ cup coconut milk

LAYER 2
¼ cup frozen acai or frozen blueberries
   or 2 tsp acai powder
leftover smoothie mixture from layer 1

LAYER 3
1 banana, frozen, peeled and cut into chunks
½ cup frozen mango chunks
± ¼ cup coconut milk

LAYER 4
leftover smoothie mixture from layer 3
½ tsp blue spirulina powder

Toppings
coconut shavings
crushed macadamia nuts
a sprig of fresh mint or edible flower

METHOD
To create the first layer, blend all the ingredients together until smooth, but still thick enough to spoon, so don't add too much coconut milk. This will also prevent the layers from leeching into one another, thereby spoiling the effect. Pour half the mixture into a jar to form the bottom layer.

For the second layer, add the acai (frozen or powdered) or frozen blueberries to the remaining half of the pink smoothie and blend until smooth. Using a spoon, pour the mixture over the first layer so that it lands 'softly', then rinse the blender well.

Now onto the third layer. Place all the ingredients into the clean blender and blend until smooth. Carefully pour half the mixture over the previous purple layer.

To make the fourth layer, combine the leftover smoothie mixture from layer 3 with the spirulina powder and blend until smooth. Pour this over the third layer. Finally, sprinkle over the toppings and enjoy.

NOTE: To achieve the angled-layer effect, pour each layer of the smoothie in at an angle, positioning the glass at the same angle in the freezer, between each layer. This takes time, so only attempt it if you want an Instagram-worthy result!

POST-WORKOUT GURU

1   1

1 SERVING

This smoothie punches above its weight when it comes to post-workout nutrition. Cinnamon and turmeric have incredible anti-inflammatory properties, the banana and dates replenish energy, and protein helps to repair muscles. Boom!

SERVES: 1 • PREP TIME: 5 min • LEVEL OF DIFFICULTY: 1/5

INGREDIENTS

1 cup almond milk
1 banana, frozen, peeled
   and cut into chunks
2 dates, pitted
½ tsp ground turmeric
¼ tsp ground ginger
¼ tsp ground cinnamon
a pinch of freshly ground
   black pepper

2 tsp plant-based protein
   powder
1 tsp maple syrup

Topping
ground turmeric,
   to sprinkle

METHOD

Pour the almond milk into the jar of a blender. Add all the other ingredients and blend until smooth. Pour into a glass and sprinkle with turmeric.

HOLISTIC HEALTH
SUPER SMOOTHIE

2   1   1

1 SERVING

This is the king and queen of healthy smoothies. It's definitely not Insta-worthy, but it's worth goes way beyond a mere image! Try it … your body will thank you.

SERVES: 1 • PREP TIME: 5 min • LEVEL OF DIFFICULTY: 1/5

INGREDIENTS

1 cup organic soy milk
1 banana, frozen, peeled
   and cut into chunks
½ cup organic berries,
   frozen (organic is
   best because berries
   are generally heavily
   sprayed with high
   levels of pesticides)
3 dates, pitted
1 heaped tsp ground
   turmeric

¼ tsp freshly ground
   black pepper
½ tsp ground cinnamon
1 cup organic baby
   spinach
1 heaped tsp nut butter
   (I like macadamia)
1 Tbsp aloe vera gel
   (the edible variety,
   not the one you put on
   your skin)

METHOD

Pour the soy milk into the jar of a blender. Add the remaining ingredients and blend until smooth. Pour into a glass.

GOLDEN LIGHT
BIRCHER MUESLI

1 BOWL

1   2

Throw out the boxes of processed cereals loaded with refined sugars and give this recipe a go instead; your tummy and body will love you. Not only will you feel fuller for longer, you will be getting a nutrient-packed breakfast filled with fibre too. And, the good news is there is hardly any prep work – no cooking required! The magic happens while you are asleep.

SERVES: 2-4 • PREP TIME: 10 min + overnight
• LEVEL OF DIFFICULTY: 1/5

INGREDIENTS

1 cup whole rolled oats
1 unpeeled apple, grated
¼ cup shredded coconut
1 cup almond milk
½ cup coconut yoghurt
½ tsp vanilla essence
3 Tbsp crushed raw
  mixed nuts

2 Tbsp maple syrup
1 Tbsp macadamia nut
  butter
1 Tbsp orange juice

Toppings
raw seeds, nuts, fresh
  fruits (your choice)

METHOD

Combine all the ingredients, except the toppings, in a bowl or resealable jar. Cover and refrigerate overnight. This muesli will last a few days if sealed well.

When ready to enjoy, serve in the jar or a bowl, then sprinkle over your favourite toppings.

THE GREEN GODDESS

1   1   1   1   **1 BOWL**

Not only will drinking this smoothie make you feel like a goddess on the inside, but carry a jar with you to the gym, kids drop-off or work, and you will look like a goddess too!

SERVES: 1 • PREP TIME: 5 min • LEVEL OF DIFFICULTY: 1/5

INGREDIENTS

1 cup coconut water

1 banana, frozen, peeled and cut into chunks

¾ cup baby spinach leaves

½ cup ice cubes

3 dates, pitted

2 Tbsp plant-based protein

1 tsp spirulina powder or fresh frozen seaweed (it's odour-free)

1 Tbsp macadamia nut butter

½ tsp ground cinnamon

1 tsp ground flaxseed

Toppings

1 tsp shaved coconut

1 tsp crushed macadamia nuts

mixed berries

edible flowers

METHOD

Pour the coconut water into the jar of a blender. Add the other ingredients, except the toppings, and blend together until smooth. Pour into a glass or a bowl and sprinkle over your choice of toppings.

WHOLESOME VEGAN GRANOLA

1 BOWL

1   1

Super simple and loaded with good fats, antioxidants and super grains, this vegan granola is a staple in my pantry. Add a little more coconut oil and maple syrup, and you can make homemade, crunchy bars that are perfect snacks for work or school lunchboxes. Or enjoy it as is, in handfuls, sprinkled over coconut yoghurt or smoothie bowls.

SERVES: 12 • PREP TIME: 25 min • LEVEL OF DIFFICULTY: 3/5

INGREDIENTS

½ cup coconut oil

½ cup maple syrup

1 cup puffed amaranth

1 cup organic rolled oats

½ cup raw macadamia nuts

½ cup raw cashew nuts

½ cup pepitas or shelled pumpkin seeds

½ cup sunflower seeds

½ cup shredded coconut
 (use desiccated if you can't find shredded)

½ cup activated buckwheat (buckinis)

¼ cup chia seeds

¼ cup hemp seeds

1 tsp ground cloves

1 tsp ground cinnamon

chopped dried papaya, dried apple or
 crystallised ginger (all optional)

METHOD

Preheat the oven to 120°C and line a baking tray (25 x 35 cm) with baking paper.

In a small pot over a medium heat, melt the coconut oil until it is completely liquid. Remove from the heat and stir in the maple syrup. Place all the remaining ingredients, except the optional dried fruit, into a bowl and mix well. Pour over the coconut oil mixture and stir until well combined and all the ingredients are coated with the oil. Spread the mixture evenly on the prepared baking tray and bake for 15–20 minutes. It can burn easily so keep checking!

Once lightly browned, remove from the oven and allow to cool completely. If you are including dried fruit, add it once the granola is completely cool. Break up and store in a well-sealed jar.

THE BIG BLUE SMOOTHIE BOWL

1   2   1   1 BOWL

SERVES: 1 • PREP TIME: 5 min
• LEVEL OF DIFFICULTY: 1/5

INGREDIENTS

1 cup coconut milk

2 bananas, frozen, peeled
   and cut into chunks

1 tsp blue spirulina powder

1 Tbsp lemon juice

1 teaspoon coconut sugar or
   maple syrup (optional)

Toppings (optional)

coconut yoghurt, desiccated coconut, granola
   (see recipe on page 52), popped quinoa, hemp
   seeds, fresh fruit or berries, edible flowers

METHOD

Pour the coconut milk into the jar of a blender.
Add all the other ingredients, except the
toppings, and blend on high until
very smooth. Pour into a bowl
and add your choice of toppings.

*'Eat and Live
Consciously'*
TAMMY FRY

THE CALCIUM BOOST
BOWL

3	1	1	1	1 BOWL

This plant-powered smoothie packs a punch in the calcium department. If you are a parent of boys (like me!), you may want to double the dose of figs and tahini, just to be sure.

SERVES: 1 • PREP TIME: 5 min
• LEVEL OF DIFFICULTY: 1/5

INGREDIENTS

½ cup almond milk
1 cup baby spinach
2 Tbsp plant-based
   protein
2 bananas, frozen,
   peeled and cut
   into chunks
1 fresh fig
2 Tbsp tahini

Toppings (optional)
shaved coconut, cacao
   nibs, raw almonds,
   raspberries, fresh
   mint, edible flowers

METHOD

Pour the almond milk into the jar of a blender. Add all the other ingredients, except the toppings, and blend on high until very smooth. Transfer to a bowl and sprinkle over your choice of toppings.

THE HAPPY DAYS
SMOOTHIE BOWL

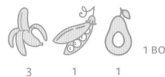

3   1   1   1 BOWL

Who doesn't want to feel good? This smoothie is a good-vibe maker. Smile!

SERVES: 1 • PREP TIME: 5 min • LEVEL OF DIFFICULTY: 1/5

INGREDIENTS

1 cup almond milk

3 Tbsp dark vegan chocolate or cacao plant-based protein powder

1 Tbsp nut butter

1 banana, frozen, peeled and cut into chunks

½ cup mixed frozen berries

½ Tbsp maple syrup

¼ tsp vanilla essence

1 Tbsp flaxseed oil

Toppings (optional)

chia seeds, pomegranate rubies, blueberries, shaved coconut, strawberries, cherries, edible flowers

METHOD

Put on your favourite playlist to get the good vibes going!

Pour the almond milk into the jar of a blender. Add all the other ingredients, except the toppings, and blend on high until very smooth. Transfer to a bowl and sprinkle over your choice of toppings.

THE BRAIN FOOD
BOWL

2   1   1   1 BOWL

So, for my post-partum friends, this smoothie is a mind-busting, brain-charging, omega-filled must-have! But it's good for the rest of you as well.

SERVES: 1 • PREP TIME: 5 min • LEVEL OF DIFFICULTY: 1/5

INGREDIENTS

½ cup almond milk

4 Tbsp dark vegan chocolate or cacao plant-based protein powder

2 bananas, frozen, peeled and cut into chunks

½ cup frozen wild blueberries

6 walnuts

1 Tbsp flaxseed oil

Toppings (optional)

chia seeds, hemp seeds, cherries, berries, shaved coconut, edible flowers

METHOD

Pour the almond milk into the jug of a blender. Add all the other ingredients, except the toppings, and blend on high until very smooth. Transfer to a bowl and sprinkle over your choice of toppings.

PINK PITAYA SMOOTHIE BOWL

2 · ½ · 1

1 BOWL

SERVES: 1 • **PREP TIME: 5 min**
• **LEVEL OF DIFFICULTY: 1/5**

INGREDIENTS

1 cup coconut milk

1 banana, frozen, peeled and cut into chunks

1 cup frozen mango chunks

¾ pink pitaya (dragon fruit), cubed
(reserve the other ¼ as a topping)

Toppings (optional)

¼ cup vegan granola (see recipe on page 52)

½ kiwi fruit, peeled and sliced

3 strawberries, hulled and sliced

reserved ¼ pink pitaya, cubed

3 fresh mint leaves

METHOD

Pour the coconut milk into the jar of a food processor. Add all the other ingredients and blend until smooth. Transfer to a jar and sprinkle over your choice of toppings.

CHAI CHIA BOWLS

1 BOWL
1

SERVES 4 • PREP TIME: 10 min • STANDING TIME: minimum 2 hours • LEVEL OF DIFFICULTY: 2/5

INGREDIENTS

2½ cups light coconut milk

2 chai and vanilla teabags (or any chai teabags, to which you can add ½ tsp vanilla essence)

3 Tbsp rice malt syrup or maple syrup

½ cup black or white chia seeds

Toppings

raw pistachios and pomegranate rubies

crumbled seed and amaranth bar
(see page 174 for recipe) (optional)

METHOD

Heat the coconut milk in a small pot over a medium heat, taking care not to burn it. Add the teabags and allow to simmer for 2–3 minutes until the flavour has infused. Stir in the syrup until well mixed. Discard the teabags and leave to cool. (Stir in the vanilla essence if using.) Add the chia seeds and stir until combined. Refrigerate for approximately 30 minutes or until the seeds have absorbed all the liquid. If the seeds become dry, top up the bowl with more coconut milk.

To serve, divide the chai chia among 4 bowls, then top with the pistachios and pomegranate rubies, and crumbled bar, if using. Decorate as desired.

'Do small things with great love'

MOTHER TERESA

OVERNIGHT OATS
FOR FOUR DAYS

   1 JAR/GLASS

1   1   1

SERVES: 1 (for 4 days) • PREP TIME: 10 min + overnight • LEVEL OF DIFFICULTY: 2/5

'Wake up ...

kick ass ...

INGREDIENTS

2 cups rolled oats

4 Tbsp maple syrup
(or sweetener of
your choice)

2 cups plant milk (oat,
almond, soy, coconut,
macadamia) or your
own homemade version

4 small jars (to serve 1)

4 Tbsp coconut yoghurt

Variations

JAR 1: 1 Tbsp nut butter
and 1 tsp cacao powder

JAR 2: 1 sliced banana
and 1 Tbsp chia seeds

JAR 3: ½ tsp spirulina
powder and a handful
of blueberries

JAR 4: ½ pink pitaya
(dragon fruit), cubed,
and a sprig of mint

METHOD

Mix together the oats, syrup or sweetener, and
plant milk. Divide the mixture among 4 jars. Add
the variation ingredients to each jar and mix
well. Seal the jars and refrigerate overnight. Drop
1 tablespoon of coconut yoghurt over each serving
before enjoying. Decorate as desired.

GOOD-FAT-KETO-NOLA

1 SMALL BOWL

2

A sugar-free, carb-free, grain-free option, this also makes for a great on-the-go or school lunchbox snack, and may be served with coconut yoghurt or coconut milk. For an extra touch of sweetness and colour, add blueberries or raspberries.

SERVES 6–8 • PREP TIME: 20 min
• LEVEL OF DIFFICULTY: 1/5

INGREDIENTS

½ cup coconut oil

½ cup walnuts

½ cup macadamia nuts

½ cup mixed seeds
   (hemp, pepita, sunflower)

½ cup shaved coconut

1 tsp ground cinnamon

¼ tsp ground cardamom

¼ tsp ground cloves

METHOD

Preheat the oven to 120°C and line a baking tray (25 x 35 cm) with baking paper.

In a small pot over a medium heat, melt the coconut oil until it is completely liquid. Combine all the remaining ingredients in a bowl, then add the melted coconut oil. Stir well to coat thoroughly. Spread the mixture in a single layer on the prepared baking tray. Bake for 12–15 minutes until the seeds and nuts are lightly browned. (They can burn quickly and easily so keep an eye on the oven and adjust the temperature and cooking time if necessary, depending on your oven.)

Once cool, store in an airtight container.

BREAKFAST CARROT CAKE

1 SERVING

2   2   2   2

Not all puddings are equal. Take this one for example, technically a cake, eaten at breakfast, no refined sugar, no dairy and nutrition in every spoonful. Breakfast doesn't get better than this.

SERVES: 2 • PREP TIME: 20 min
• COOKING TIME: 10 min • LEVEL OF DIFFICULTY: 2/5

INGREDIENTS

1 cup coconut milk

1 cup water

1 cup rolled oats

2 cups peeled and grated carrots

2 bananas, mashed

4 Tbsp raisins or dried goji berries

2 Tbsp maple syrup

1 tsp ground cinnamon

1 tsp vanilla spice or vanilla essence

½ tsp ground ginger

½ tsp ground nutmeg

½ tsp ground cloves

½ cup coconut cream

Toppings

shaved coconut, maple syrup (to taste), pineapple pieces

METHOD

In a small pot over a medium heat, bring the milk and water to a simmer. Add the oats and bring to a slow boil, then reduce the heat and allow to simmer for 3 minutes. Add the grated carrots, bananas and raisins or berries, as well as the maple syrup, vanilla essence and spices. Cook for another 3–5 minutes. Pour in the coconut cream and stir well, allowing to simmer for approximately 5 minutes until the liquid is absorbed and a thick consistency is reached.

Add the topings and decorate as desired. Enjoy the 'cake' warm.

TOFU SCRAMBLE

1 SERVING

1   1   1

SERVES: 2–4 • PREP TIME: 10 min • COOKING TIME: 15 min • LEVEL OF DIFFICULTY: 2/5

INGREDIENTS

1 Tbsp coconut oil

1 medium brown onion, diced

1 red pepper, deseeded and diced

6–8 mushrooms, sliced

2 cups organic baby spinach

1 block organic tofu (I prefer firm), crumbled

¼ tsp ground turmeric

a pinch of ground smoky paprika

a pinch of Indian black salt (this smells exactly like egg, so if you'd prefer, replace with ¼ tsp garlic powder, ¼ tsp onion powder and ¼ tsp Himalayan salt)

1 avocado, sliced

METHOD

In a frying pan, heat the coconut oil over a medium-high heat. Sauté the onion, red pepper and mushrooms for 5 minutes. Add the spinach and tofu, then cook for another 5 minutes. Add the turmeric, paprika and salt and cook for 2 more minutes. Serve with sliced avocado.

PROTEIN-PACKED
CHICKPEA OMELETTE

1 1 2 1

1 OMELETTE

SERVES: 2 • PREP TIME: 5 min
• COOKING TIME: 5 min • LEVEL OF DIFFICULTY: 2/5

INGREDIENTS

Batter

1½ cups chickpea flour
½ cup coconut milk
¼ cup water, room
   temperature (or more
   if the batter is too thick)
½ tsp baking powder
½ tsp ground smoked
   paprika
1 tsp ground turmeric
½ tsp fine salt (for an
   eggier flavour use
   Indian salt)

1 Tbsp tamari or vegan
   miso paste
2 Tbsp extra virgin olive oil

Filling

beans, tofu, spinach,
   cherry tomatoes, onion,
   mushroom, garlic,
   red cabbage, lightly
   sautéed (your choice)

Toppings

grated vegan cheese,
   fresh basil

METHOD

Using a whisk, combine all the batter ingredients,
except the olive oil, until smooth. Heat 1 Tbsp olive
oil in a pan over a medium heat, then pour in half
the batter, allowing it to spread out and bubble
like a pancake. Once bubbles appear on the surface
(2–4 minutes), turn over to cook both sides equally.

Serve the omelettes topped or filled with the
filling, then sprinkle over the vegan cheese and basil.

DECONSTRUCTED APPLE AND BLUEBERRY BREAKFAST CRUMBLE

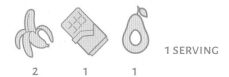

2   1   1   1 SERVING

A healthy twist on a traditional dish. Getting jiggy with it ... This is delicious, whether served for breakfast or for dessert.

SERVES: 2–4 • PREP TIME: 15 min • COOKING TIME: 25 min • LEVEL OF DIFFICULTY: 3/5

INGREDIENTS

Filling

1 Tbsp coconut oil

3 unpeeled Pink Lady apples, cut into small cubes

1 Tbsp maple syrup

1 cup blueberries

1 tsp grated orange zest

juice of 1 orange

1 tsp vanilla essence

Crumble

2 Tbsp coconut oil

¼ cup shaved coconut

¼ cup popped quinoa or popped amaranth

¼ cup rolled oats, chopped

2 Tbsp crushed macadamia nuts

1 tsp ground cinnamon

2 tsp coconut sugar

Serve with

fresh mint

3 Tbsp coconut yoghurt

METHOD

Preheat the oven to 160°C and grease a medium-sized, ovenproof dish with coconut oil or cooking spray.

To prepare the filling, heat the coconut oil in a medium-sized, heavy-based pan over a medium heat. Add the apples and cook for 6 minutes. Add the maple syrup and cook for another 4 minutes, stirring continuously. Finally, mix in the blueberries, orange zest and orange juice. Remove from the heat, stir in the vanilla essence and set aside.

Next, prepare the crumble by combining all the crumble ingredients in a small mixing bowl. Spoon the fruit mixture into the ovenproof dish and sprinkle over the crumble. Bake for 25–30 minutes. Garnish with the mint and serve with the coconut yoghurt.

GLAZED AND GRILLED FRUIT SKEWERS
WITH
CHOCOLATE SAUCE

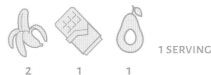

2   1   1

1 SERVING

SERVES: 4 • PREP TIME: 15 min • LEVEL OF DIFFICULTY: 2/5

INGREDIENTS

4–6 wooden skewers

Syrup sauce

1 Tbsp maple syrup
a pinch of chilli flakes or cayenne pepper
½ fresh lemon, juiced
½ tsp vanilla extract

Fruit skewers

1 pineapple, peeled and cut into 2–3 cm chunks
1 punnet strawberries, washed, hulled and halved
2 peaches, washed and cut into 2–3 cm chunks
2 pears, washed and cut into 2–3 cm chunks

Chocolate sauce

2 Tbsp cocoa powder
2 Tbsp maple syrup
2 Tbsp almond milk
2 Tbsp smooth nut butter
1 tsp vanilla extract

Toppings

coconut flakes, pomegranate rubies

METHOD

Soak the wooden skewers in cold water for 10 minutes to prevent them from burning. Preheat the grill on high.

In a small bowl, mix together the maple syrup, chilli flakes or cayenne pepper, lemon juice and vanilla extract. Coat the chunks of pineapple, strawberry, peach and pear with the syrup sauce, then thread the chunks onto the skewers. Arrange the skewers next to one another in a single layer on a baking sheet under the preheated grill for 10 minutes, turning every now and then. Check them regularly to make sure they don't char.

Meanwhile, combine all the ingredients for the chocolate sauce in a small saucepan over a low heat. Using a stick blender or food processor, blend until smooth. Store the sauce in the fridge where it will thicken.

Serve the fruit skewers dipped in the chocolate sauce, and then sprinkle with some coconut flakes and pomegranate rubies.

CHOCOLATE-CHIP PROTEIN PANCAKES
WITH VANILLA
BLUEBERRY CHIA SEED JAM

1	½	1

2 PANCAKES

SERVES: 2 • PREP TIME: 10 min

• COOKING TIME: Varies, depending on the number of pans you use • LEVEL OF DIFFICULTY: 3/5

INGREDIENTS

Vanilla blueberry chia seed jam

3 cups fresh blueberries

3 Tbsp pure maple syrup, or to taste

2 Tbsp water

2 Tbsp chia seeds

½ tsp vanilla essence

Pancakes

1 cup spelt flour (or all-purpose flour if you
    don't have spelt)

¼ cup vegan vanilla protein powder

2 tsp baking powder

½ tsp ground cinnamon

a pinch of salt

½ cup almond milk

½ cup water

3 Tbsp rice malt syrup or maple syrup

1 tsp lemon juice

1 tsp vanilla essence

3 Tbsp vegan dark chocolate chips

1 tsp coconut oil

To serve

sliced bananas

2 Tbsp nut butter

METHOD

For the pancakes, add the flour, protein powder, baking powder, cinnamon and salt to a medium-sized bowl, then whisk to mix and aerate. In a separate bowl and using a clean whisk, combine the almond milk, water, syrup, lemon juice and vanilla essence. Pour this mixture into the dry mixture and mix until smooth. Stir in the chocolate chips.

Heat a non-stick pan and add the coconut oil. Once the pan is hot, pour the pancake mixture into the pan – the smaller the pancakes the easier it is to flip them, so I suggest around a quarter cup of the mixture per pancake or 10 cm diameter. Using a spatula, flip the pancake once it starts to bubble on the surface (1–2 minutes) and the base is slightly firm. Stack the pancakes on a plate and pour over the jam. Serve with sliced bananas and blobs of nut butter.

For the jam, bring the blueberries, maple syrup and water to a boil in a medium-sized, non-stick pot, over a medium heat, stirring frequently. Reduce the heat to a simmer and allow to cook for about 5 minutes. Lightly mash the blueberries with a potato masher or fork, leaving some semi whole for texture.

Stir in the chia seeds until well combined and cook until the mixture reduces and thickens to the desired consistency (about 10 minutes). Stir frequently to prevent it from sticking to the pot. Once the jam is thick, remove from the heat and stir in the vanilla essence. Add more maple syrup if desired.

Store in the fridge until ready to be served with the pancakes. The jam should keep for at least a week in an air-tight container. There's likely to be some over, which you can keep for another meal.

LIGHT MEALS
AND
SHARING PLATES

VIETNAMESE RICE PAPER ROLLS
WITH HOISIN-PEANUT
DIPPING SAUCE

1   1   1

1 SERVING = 4 ROLLS

Summery, light, fresh and tasty, these rolls are low in calories, but pack a flavour punch. They're perfect for picnics on the beach or birthday parties.

SERVES: 4 • PREP TIME: 30 min • COOKING TIME: 3–5 min • LEVEL OF DIFFICULTY: 4/5

INGREDIENTS

Rice paper rolls

120 g rice vermicelli

16 small rice paper wrappers

2 Tbsp finely chopped fresh basil

6 Tbsp finely chopped fresh mint

6 Tbsp finely chopped fresh coriander

2 carrots, finely julienned

4 lettuce leaves, thinly sliced

1 punnet sprouts (your choice), washed

¼ cup pickled sushi ginger

2 avocados, sliced

edible flowers

Hoisin-peanut dipping sauce

6 Tbsp hoisin sauce

¼ cup peanut butter

1 tsp finely chopped red chillies

1 clove garlic, crushed

METHOD

Boil the rice vermicelli for 3–5 minutes. Rinse thoroughly with cold water and drain well so they don't stick together, then set aside. Fill a large bowl with room temperature water. Dip a wrapper into the water for 3–5 seconds, just to soften enough to make it pliable. Place the wrapper on a plate and spoon 2 heaped tablespoons of vermicelli, some basil, mint, coriander, carrots, lettuce, sprouts and ginger in a row across the centre, leaving a few centimetres of the wrapper clear on each side. Lay the avocado slices and edible flowers over the other filling. Fold in the clear sides of wrapper, then tightly roll to enclose the filling. Repeat with the remaining wrappers and filling.

To make the dipping sauce, mix all the ingredients together. If necessary, add a little water. Serve the rice paper rolls cold with the dipping sauce.

LOADED HOMEMADE NACHOS

1 SERVING

1   1   1   2

SERVES: 3 • PREPARATION TIME: 15 min • COOKING TIME: 12 min • LEVEL OF DIFFICULTY: 2/5

INGREDIENTS

3 soft flour tortillas or wraps

1 Tbsp olive oil

1 tsp smoky paprika

1 tsp ground coriander

½ tsp ground cumin

2 tsp salt

2 plant-based schnitzels (e.g. Fry's)

Guacamole

2 avocados, mashed

½ red onion, diced

2 cloves garlic, minced

a handful of fresh coriander, roughly chopped

juice of 1 lime

salt to taste

Tomato salsa

2 medium tomatoes, skinned and finely chopped

¼ red onion, very finely chopped

1 small clove garlic, chopped

a splash of white wine vinegar

juice of ½ lime

a handful of fresh coriander, roughly chopped

To serve

black olives, depipped

1 x 400 g can black beans, drained and rinsed

lime wedges

METHOD

Preheat the oven to 180°C. Cut the tortillas or wraps into 6 small triangles (like pizza wedges). Brush the triangles with the olive oil and sprinkle with the paprika, coriander, cumin and salt. Arrange the tortilla triangles and schnitzels on a baking tray and bake in the oven for 3–5 minutes, taking care not to burn them. Remove the tortilla chips but return the schnitzels to the oven for another 5 minutes. Once the schnitzels are done, slice them into strips.

To make the guacamole, combine all the ingredients, except the salt, in a bowl, then season to taste.

For the salsa, combine all the ingredients in a small bowl. Place the tortilla chips in a bowl and top them with the schnitzel strips.

Serve with the guacamole, tomato salsa, black olives, black beans and lime wedges. You could also serve this dish with vegan sour cream (see recipe on page 98).

INDONESIAN COLESLAW
WITH STICKY
SESAME DRESSING

			1 SERVING
1	2	2	

A deliciously fresh crunchy salad that goes with almost any plant protein, so add tempeh, tofu or plant-based 'chicken' for a colourful dish. Eat the Rainbow!

SERVES: 4–6 (as a side or a main with added protein) • PREP TIME: 15 min • LEVEL OF DIFFICULTY: 1/5

INGREDIENTS

Salad

¼ head red cabbage, finely sliced

salt

1 red pepper, finely sliced or julienned

3 spring onions, finely sliced

a handful of fresh coriander, finely chopped

2 carrots, grated

½ cup sprouts (your choice)

Sticky sesame dressing

3 Tbsp rice vinegar

2 Tbsp tamari

2 Tbsp coconut sugar

1 Tbsp almond butter

1 Tbsp sesame oil

2 tsp minced fresh ginger

1 clove garlic, minced

Topping

¼ cup chopped dry-roasted almonds

¼ cup black sesame seeds

METHOD

For the salad base, place the cabbage in a colander or strainer and sprinkle with salt. Allow to stand for 10 minutes, then rinse, drain and pat dry thoroughly. In a medium-sized bowl, toss the cabbage with the remaining salad ingredients.

Whisk the dressing ingredients and pour over the salad. Scatter the almonds and sesame seeds over the top.

HOMEMADE CORN TORTILLAS
WITH PINEAPPLE
AND BLACK BEAN SALSA

(2 TORTILLAS)　　　　　　　(SALSA)　　1 SERVING

1　　　　　　1　　1　　1

Super simple, three ingredients, a few minutes, loads of delicious meals. Homemade tortillas are not only easy to make, but also include none of the nasties often found in similar products in supermarkets.

MAKES: 12–14 tortillas • PREP TIME: 20 min • COOKING TIME: 30 min • LEVEL OF DIFFICULTY: 2/5

INGREDIENTS

Corn tortillas
2 cups masa harina
½ tsp fine Himalayan salt
1½ cups warm water

Salsa
½ pineapple, peeled and sliced
　　into 2 cm rings

1 red pepper, deseeded and
　　quartered
1 x 400 g can black beans, drained
　　and rinsed
½ cup finely chopped fresh
　　coriander
2 cm piece fresh ginger, grated
½ red onion, finely diced
3 spring onions, thinly sliced

1 Tbsp sesame oil
1 tsp sesame seeds
1 Tbsp coconut sugar
2 Tbsp lime juice
pink Himalayan salt to taste
freshly ground black pepper to
　　taste

METHOD

For the corn tortillas, add the masa harina and salt to a mixing bowl. Add 1 cup of the warm water and stir until the water is absorbed. Add the remaining water slowly, stirring until a ball forms. Knead the dough by hand on a clean surface for about 3 minutes. You may need a little more or less water for the right consistency; the dough shouldn't stick to your hands but if it does, add more masa harina. Break the dough into ping pong-sized balls. To flatten them, you will need food-grade plastic wrap, a toasted sandwich press and a large casserole dish or a rolling pin. Place each ball between 2 sheets of plastic wrap (this will prevent the tortilla from sticking to surfaces) and press or use a rolling pin to roll to 2 mm thickness. Heat a non-stick pan. Carefully peel the plastic wrap from the tortillas and place them in the pan, cooking for 1–2 minutes per side. Serve immediately or store in the fridge. If reheating, sprinkle a few drops of water over the tortilla while it is in the pan.

　　For the salsa, heat the grill to medium-high. Place the pineapple and red pepper under the grill and cook until slightly softened, caramelised and charred. When ready, place in the fridge. Once cooled, dice into small cubes. Add the pineapple and red pepper to a medium-sized bowl, along with the remaining ingredients and mix well.

SIMPLE BABY MARROW FRITTERS

1 SERVING – 2 FRITTERS

Fritters can be made with a variety of veggie and spice combinations. I think they could almost be the fairy godmother of the kitchen ... dress them up or down with a variety of garnishes or buns to make mini sliders ... the options are endless.

SERVES: 4–6 • PREP TIME: 20 min
• COOKING TIME: Depends on the number of pans you have! • LEVEL OF DIFFICULTY: 4/5

INGREDIENTS

8–10 medium baby marrows, washed and grated

3 spring onions, thinly sliced

1 tsp fine salt

2 heaped Tbsp cornflour

1 tsp dried oregano, rubbed

1 tsp freshly ground black pepper

1 tsp ground turmeric

1 tsp smoky paprika

2 cloves garlic, crushed

1 cup wholewheat flour or chickpea flour (besan)
    for a gluten-free option

¼ cup olive oil

METHOD

Place the baby marrows and spring onions in a colander. Sprinkle over the salt and set aside for 10 minutes until softened. In a large bowl, mix the cornflour with 3 tablespoons of water until a smooth paste is formed (this replaces egg as a binding agent). Add the oregano, pepper, turmeric and paprika to the cornflour mixture.

Take handfuls of grated baby marrow and spring onions and squeeze to remove excess water. Place them in the bowl with the spiced cornflour mixture and add the garlic. Add enough flour to form a thick batter (this will depend on the type of flour used). Heat the oil in a non-stick pan. To test if it's hot enough, drop a tiny ball of batter into the oil; it should sizzle. Drop spoonfuls of batter in the oil, pressing down lightly to form fritters. Turn once or twice until both sides are lightly browned and crisped. Remove from oil and place on paper towel to drain.

Garnish as desired and serve with a dipping sauce of your choice.

'SUSHI' JARS
WITH CASHEW WASABI CREAM

1 SERVING = (WITH VEGAN PRAWNS)

1   1   1   1   1

SERVES: 6 (or 2 medium-sized jars) • **PREP TIME:** 20 min
• **COOKING TIME:** 15 min (+10 min with 'prawns') • **LEVEL OF DIFFICULTY:** 2/5

INGREDIENTS

2 sterilised jars

¼ red cabbage, shredded

2 carrots, grated

1 cup edamame beans, shelled

¼ cup sushi ginger

1 avocado, sliced

¼ cup wakame seaweed

juice of 1 lime

½ pack vegan prawn-style pieces
   (optional) (e.g. Fry's)

½ cup teriyaki sauce (store bought or see
   recipe opposite)

Quinoa base

1 cup white quinoa

2 cups water

4 Tbsp rice vinegar

2 Tbsp white sugar

½ Tbsp pink Himalayan salt

Cashew wasabi cream

½ cup raw cashews, soaked overnight and well drained

1 Tbsp wasabi paste or 2 tsp wasabi powder

½ tsp salt

2 tsp lime juice

¼ cup water (or more depending on your blender)

METHOD

For the quinoa base, wash the quinoa under cold, running water until the water runs clear. Add the quinoa and water to a saucepan over a high heat, stirring occasionally, until it boils. Reduce the heat to low and simmer, uncovered, for 10–12 minutes. Combine the vinegar, sugar and salt in a small bowl. Once the quinoa is cooked, transfer it to a ceramic or plastic bowl and fold in the vinegar mixture. Place in the fridge to cool.

Add all the cashew wasabi cream ingredients to a blender, gradually adding the water. Blend for 30 seconds until smooth and creamy.

To assemble, place a quarter cup of the quinoa mixture at the bottom of a sterilised jar. Follow this with a layer of the cabbage, carrots, beans, ginger, avocado and wakame seaweed. Repeat for the second jar. Squeeze the lime over the salad layers. Seal and refrigerate for up to 3 days. When ready to serve, grill the prawn-style pieces. Skewer the 'prawns' and dip them into the cashew wasabi cream, then add them to the salad jars. Serve, drizzled with 2–3 Tbsp of the teriyaki sauce.

HOMEMADE TERIYAKI SAUCE

INGREDIENTS

1 cup naturally brewed soy sauce

100 ml sake

100 ml mirin

50 ml water

60 g coconut sugar

METHOD

In a small saucepan, mix all the ingredients together.

Heat over medium heat and bring to the boil, then gently simmer for 15 minutes or until slightly thickened. The 'sushi jar' only requires 120 ml of the sauce, but it's great to keep in a sealed bottle in the fridge to enjoy with other dishes.

'MEXICAN-BUDDHA' BOWL

1   1½   2   1

1 SERVING

SERVES: 2–4 • PREP TIME: 15 min • COOKING TIME: 30 min • LEVEL OF DIFFICULTY: 1/5

INGREDIENTS

Salsa

½ red onion, chopped

½ pineapple, peeled and roughly chopped

1 tomato, skinned and chopped

½ tsp fine Himalayan salt

juice of ½ lime (keep the rest for the toppings)

a handful of fresh coriander, chopped

Bowl

½ x 400 g can chickpeas, rinsed, drained and dried

2 cups peeled and cubed butternut

1 Tbsp extra virgin olive oil

1 tsp ground cumin

½ tsp ground cinnamon

salt and pepper, to taste

1½ cups uncooked quinoa, rinsed

3 cups water

2 cloves garlic, crushed

1 brown onion, sliced

1 red pepper, sliced

½ tsp chipotle chilli powder (or for a milder version ½ tsp smoky paprika and ½ tsp ground cumin)

½ tsp Himalayan salt

½ x 400 g can black beans, rinsed and drained

½ cup cooked corn (sliced off the cob) or canned whole kernel corn, drained

1 avocado, sliced

1–2 jalapeños, sliced

Toppings

hemp seeds, lime wedges

METHOD

First make the salsa. Combine all the ingredients in a bowl.

Preheat the oven to 200°C. Line a baking tray with baking paper. Place the chickpeas and butternut in a bowl, then add the oil, cumin and cinnamon. Toss to coat evenly. Season with salt and pepper. Spread the chickpeas and butternut on the prepared baking tray and roast for 30 minutes.

Boil the quinoa in the water for 15–18 minutes until soft. Drain any excess water. Heat some oil in a pan. Add the garlic, onion, red pepper, chipotle powder and Himalayan salt and fry for about 5 minutes, until the onions are soft and translucent. Remove and set onion mixture aside. Add the black beans and corn to the same pan and fry for 3–5 minutes over high heat to slightly char. Set aside to cool. Add the quinoa mixture to a bowl, followed by the onion mixture, black beans and corn, the roasted chickpeas and butternut, avocado slices, sliced jalapeños and toppings. Serve with the salsa.

'Three things cannot hide for long:
the sun, the moon and the truth'
BUDDHA

PUMPKIN AND COCONUT
WINTER SOUP

1   ½   1 SERVING = 1 BOWL

There is nothing quite like cold, rainy days, huddled around a fire, a bowl of warm soup with crusty bread in your hands. It is honestly magical. Unless, of course, you are on the beach with the warm sun on your back and salt in your hair. That might just beat the rainy day!

SERVES: 4 • PREP TIME: 10 min • COOKING TIME: 30 min • LEVEL OF DIFFICULTY: 2/4

INGREDIENTS

3 Tbsp extra virgin olive oil

1 large brown onion, chopped

2 cloves garlic, crushed

3 cm piece fresh ginger, grated

4 cups peeled and cubed (2 cm cubes) pumpkin

2 cups vegetable stock (see recipe on page 140)

2 cups coconut milk

a sprig of fresh rosemary

1 bunch fresh flat-leaf parsley

fine salt to taste

freshly ground black pepper to taste

½ cup coconut cream

vegan parmesan (see page 155)

METHOD

Heat the olive oil in a large pot and lightly sauté the onion until translucent. Add the garlic and ginger, and sauté for 2 minutes. Add the pumpkin and fry for 5–8 minutes until the pumpkin is slightly browned at the edges. Pour in the stock and coconut milk, and bring to a simmer. Allow to simmer, covered, for 20–25 minutes until the pumpkin is tender. Stir in the herbs for the last 5 minutes of simmering, then discard the rosemary. Using a stick blender, blend until smooth. Season with salt and pepper. Add the coconut cream and increase the heat, but do not boil.

Sprinkle over the vegan parmesan and garnish as desired. Serve with beer bread (see page 116). If you have any leftover soup, it will keep well in small containers in the freezer.

ROASTED BUTTERNUT, BEETROOT
AND CRISPY SAGE TART

1 SERVING

1   2

Sunday lunches with friends or movie nights in, this tart looks incredible served with a side salad. The hot water crust is one of the oldest forms of pastry and is usually baked freeform without a dish or just rolled out like a pizza base topped with veggies. Like this one!

SERVES: 4–6 • PREP TIME: 15 min • COOKING TIME: 60 min • LEVEL OF DIFFICULTY: 4/5

INGREDIENTS

Topping

2 cups (± 400 g) baby beetroots, washed

½ butternut (225–275 g), peeled and cubed

2 Tbsp apple cider vinegar

1 Tbsp rice malt syrup

½ tsp fine Himalayan salt

½ tsp freshly ground black pepper

Hot water pastry crust

100 g vegan butter or margarine

80 ml water, room temperature

1½ cups wholemeal spelt flour

½ tsp fine Himalayan salt

1 Tbsp finely chopped fresh sage

Topping

1 Tbsp extra virgin olive oil

4–6 sprigs fresh sage

¼ cup roughly chopped walnuts

METHOD

Heat the oven to 200°C. Line 1 or 2 standard baking trays with foil. Beetroots and butternut may be placed on the same tray, but 2 trays are preferable as these vegetable do not necessarily cook for the same length of time. Trim the leaves and upper stems of the beetroots, leaving 2 cm of the stem intact. Scrub (don't peel) the skin of the beetroots, then halve them. If the beetroots are large, cut them into smaller pieces or slices. In a medium-sized bowl, combine the vinegar, syrup, salt and pepper, and toss with the beetroot. Arrange the butternut and beetroots onto the tray/s and roast for 30–40 minutes until tender, but not overcooked (use a skewer to test).

Meanwhile, place the vegan butter and water in a pot and bring to a boil. Add the flour, salt and sage and mix until the dough comes together. Remove the dough from the pot and knead for a few minutes, until smooth. Roll out on a sheet of baking paper to form a large 'pizza' shape. Place in the oven with the vegetables for 10–15 minutes. Try to have the vegetables and pastry ready at the same time. Top the pastry with the roasted vegetables and return to the oven for another 20 minutes until the base is cooked through and slightly browned.

To prepare the topping, heat the oil in a pan and lightly sauté the sage and walnuts for 1 minute. Sprinkle the tart with the crisped sage and roasted walnuts.

FAMILY DINNERS

ROASTED CAULIFLOWER BIRYANI

1   1   1   1 SERVING

This biryani, with a modern twist, is to celebrate my Durban roots.

SERVES: 6–8 • PREP TIME: 15 min • COOKING TIME: 30 min • LEVEL OF DIFFICULTY: 3/5

INGREDIENTS

1 cauliflower, cut into 2 cm florets

1 Tbsp extra virgin olive oil

½ tsp ground turmeric

¼ tsp ground cinnamon

¼ tsp fine salt

¼ tsp freshly ground black pepper

1 medium brown onion, thinly sliced

2 carrots, thinly sliced

2 baby marrows, thinly sliced

1 Tbsp medium or hot curry powder (or make your own using ground ginger, ground coriander, ground cumin, turmeric, chilli flakes and garam masala)

2 cups uncooked brown or white basmati rice

4 cups vegetable stock (from 2 stock cubes or vegetable stock paste, see recipe on page 140)

½ cup roughly chopped fresh coriander, plus extra to garnish

½ cup roughly chopped roasted almonds

1 cup coconut yoghurt

METHOD

Preheat the oven to 200°C and line a standard baking tray with baking paper.

Place the cauliflower on the tray and brush with olive oil. Sprinkle over the turmeric, cinnamon, salt and pepper, and stir well to coat. Roast in the oven for 15–20 minutes, until tender and slightly browned on the edges.

Add a drizzle of olive oil to a large pan over a medium to high heat. Add the onion, carrots and baby marrows to the pan and stir for approximately 5 minutes until the onions are translucent. Stir in the curry powder for 1 minute, taking care not to burn the spice.

Add the rice to the pan and stir until coated. Pour in the stock and bring the mixture to a boil. Reduce the heat to low, cover and simmer for 15–20 minutes, until the rice is tender. Stir through the roasted cauliflower, coriander and almonds. Serve with a dollop of coconut yoghurt and garnish with the extra coriander.

NOTE: If you precook the rice the day before and leave it to chill completely, the texture will be even better. Leftover rice works really well!

CASHEW FRIED RICE
WITH CRISPY BAKED TOFU

1 SERVING

1   1   1   1

Trust me – you will need to make an extra-large batch. This rice is great packed into a flask for school lunches, after-school snack or even heated up for next-day dinners. It is nutritionally well balanced and satisfying. Full bellies and smiles = happy Mom!

SERVES: 4–6 • PREP TIME: 10 min • COOKING TIME: 40 min • LEVEL OF DIFFICULTY: 3/5

INGREDIENTS

4 cups water

2 cups uncooked brown rice

2 cups firm tofu, pressed

1 Tbsp sesame oil

2 cloves garlic, crushed

1 brown onion, finely chopped

3 spring onions, sliced

1 tsp smoky paprika

1 red pepper, diced

1 carrot, diced

½ cup sugar snap peas, sliced
   diagonally

½ cup roasted cashew nuts

1 Tbsp soy sauce or tamari or
   to taste

1 long red chilli, deseeded and
   chopped (optional)

Sauce

5 Tbsp soy sauce or tamari

2 Tbsp smooth nut butter

3 Tbsp maple syrup

1 clove garlic, crushed

METHOD

Preheat the oven to 180°C and lightly grease a baking tray with cooking spray or coconut oil. Bring the water to the boil and add the brown rice. Leave to simmer, uncovered, for 25–30 minutes. Try to avoid stirring the rice. Meanwhile, wrap the tofu in absorbent paper towel and place something heavy on top to squeeze out the water. Cut the tofu into 2 cm cubes and arrange them in a single layer on the prepared baking tray. Bake for 25 minutes, or until golden brown. Turn once during baking so that they brown on both sides.

While the tofu is baking, heat the sesame oil over a medium-high heat in a large pan. Add the garlic, onion, spring onions and paprika and lightly sauté for 3–4 minutes. Add the red pepper, carrot, peas and cashew nuts, and sauté for a further 3 minutes.

To make the sauce, combine the ingredients in a small bowl and mix well. Place the baked tofu in a bowl and pour over the sauce. Mix well until the tofu is evenly coated. Once the rice is tender, rinse and drain in a colander or sieve until completely cool. Ensure that all the water is drained. Add the rice and tofu to the sautéed vegetables in the pan, mix and fry for 4 minutes over a high heat. Add soy sauce or tamari to taste. Serve, topped with chopped fresh chillies, if using.

UNEARTHED MEXICAN SWEET POTATOES

2   1   1   1 SERVING (½ POTATO)   ½   WITH ¼ CUP VEGAN SOUR CREAM

A family meal that could easily become a weekday staple. As they say in Mexico, *Buen provecho!*

SERVES: 4 • PREP TIME: 10 min • COOKING TIME: 45 min • LEVEL OF DIFFICULTY: 3/5

INGREDIENTS

4 whole sweet potatoes, scrubbed

3 tsp extra virgin olive oil

1 tsp Himalayan salt, crushed

1 x 400 g can sweetcorn, drained or
   2 fresh corn cobs

1 tsp ground cumin

1 tsp smoky paprika

1 x 400 g can black beans (or red
   kidney beans), drained and rinsed

1 red pepper, diced

a few sprigs fresh coriander

1 avocado, mashed

1 cup vegan sour cream
   (see below)

juice of 1 lime

METHOD

Preheat the oven to 180°C. Brush each sweet potato with 1 teaspoon of olive oil and sprinkle with salt. Place the potatoes on a baking sheet and bake for approximately 40 minutes, until soft in the centre. If using fresh corn cobs, steam for 20 minutes until tender, then slice off the corn and set aside. For added smokiness, char the corn after steaming.

    Meanwhile, heat a medium-sized saucepan, add 1 teaspoon of olive oil, as well as the cumin and paprika. Fry for 30 seconds until fragrant. Add the beans, red pepper and corn. Fry for 6 minutes, then set aside. Slice the baked sweet potatoes lengthways and fill with the bean, pepper and corn mixture. (You can hollow them out slightly to make the filling fit better, if necessary). Serve with coriander, avocado and vegan sour cream. Squeeze lime over the top, to taste.

VEGAN SOUR CREAM

MAKES: ± 1½ cups • PREP TIME: 4 hours, soaking + 10 min • LEVEL OF DIFFICULTY: 1/5

INGREDIENTS

1 cup raw cashew nuts,
   soaked for 4 hours

½ cup water

1 tsp apple cider vinegar

¼ tsp Dijon mustard

1 Tbsp lemon juice

fine Himalayan salt
   to taste

METHOD

Drain and rinse cashew the nuts. In a blender, blend the nuts, water, vinegar, mustard, lemon juice and salt until smooth and creamy. Serve immediately or store in an airtight container in the fridge for up to 4 days.

WEST AFRICAN COCONUT CURRY

1 SERVING

1 SERVING WITH RICE

Inspired by the peanut-based curries of West Africa, this hearty curry will have you dishing up seconds.

SERVES: 6–8 • PREP TIME: 20 min • COOKING TIME: 30 min • LEVEL OF DIFFICULTY: 2/5

INGREDIENTS

1 Tbsp coconut oil

1 medium brown onion, chopped

2 cm piece fresh ginger, grated

1 clove garlic, crushed

1 Tbsp garam masala

1 tsp ground coriander

3 cups coconut milk

1 tsp ground turmeric

1 red chilli, deseeded and sliced into rings (optional)

2½ cups peeled and cubed sweet potatoes

2 cups peeled and cubed butternut

½ red pepper, sliced into 1 cm strips

3 cups vegetable stock (see recipe on page 140)

¼ cup crunchy peanut butter

a handful fresh coriander

salt and pepper to taste

To serve

Rice, bread, crushed peanuts, toasted wraps (optional)

METHOD

In a large saucepan, heat the coconut oil over a medium heat. Add the onion, ginger, garlic, garam masala and ground coriander, then lightly sauté for 3–5 minutes taking care not to burn the spices (they really just need to be lightly toasted, so stir continuously and add a tablespoon of water if they begin to brown too much).

Add the coconut milk, turmeric, chilli, sweet potatoes, butternut, red pepper, stock and peanut butter. Bring to a simmer over a low heat and leave to simmer, uncovered, for 20–30 minutes, or until the vegetables are tender. Add the fresh coriander for the last 10 minutes, but reserve some as garnish. Season with salt and pepper.

Serve with rice of your choice, homemade beer bread, crushed peanuts or toasted wraps.

CREAMY VEGETABLE KORMA

1   2   1 SERVING

Comfort food in all its glory. A perfect korma should be deliciously creamy and nutty with just the right amount of spice. This recipe provides some scope to make it your own, so before throwing out those '1-day-to-go' veggies, head over to this page and get cooking, but remember to adjust the cooking time to whatever veg you choose. I hope you'll love this vegan version as much as my kids do!

SERVES: 4–6 • PREP TIME: 10 min • COOKING TIME: 20 min • LEVEL OF DIFFICULTY: 3/5

INGREDIENTS

2 Tbsp coconut oil

2 medium brown onions, chopped

2 cloves garlic, crushed

3 cm piece fresh ginger, grated

1 tsp ground cumin

2 Tbsp medium garam masala

1 tsp ground turmeric

2 sweet potatoes, cubed

½ head broccoli (150–200 g),
   broken into florets

1 cup cubed butternut (1–2 cm cubes)

1 red pepper, deseeded and diced

1 long red chilli, chopped

1 cup coconut milk (or ½ cup
   coconut milk and ½ cup coconut
   cream for a richer korma)

1½ cups vegetable stock
   (see recipe for vegetable stock
   paste on page 140)

2 tsp coconut sugar

2 Tbsp fresh lime juice

¾ cup frozen peas

15–20 cashew nuts, soaked in
   warm water, then drained

2 Tbsp sesame seeds

½ cup coconut yoghurt

1 tsp salt or to taste

Garnish

chopped fresh coriander

¼ cup roasted cashew nuts

¼ cup coconut flakes, toasted

METHOD

Heat the coconut oil in a heavy-bottomed saucepan over a medium-high heat. Add the onions and fry for 5–8 minutes until the onions just start to brown. Add the garlic and ginger, and sauté over a medium heat for 3–5 minutes. Stir in the cumin, garam masala and turmeric, then sauté until the onions have caramelised. Add the sweet potatoes, broccoli, butternut, red pepper and chilli, and stir over a medium heat for 2–4 minutes until the vegetables are lightly coated with the spices.

Pour in the coconut milk, stock, sugar and lime juice, and simmer for 12–15 minutes, making sure all the vegetables are cooked through and tender. Stir in the peas and bring up to a simmer again. Place the cashew nuts, sesame seeds and yoghurt in the bowl of a blender (or use an immersion blender) and blitz together to create a nut paste. Stir the nut paste into the korma and simmer for another 3–5 minutes. Remove from the heat and season to taste.

Garnish with the coriander, cashew nuts and coconut flakes.

'In a gentle way,
you can shake the world'

MAHATMA GANDHI

THAI GREEN CURRY

(WITH TOFU)

1   1   1

(WITH RICE)

1   1   1   1

This is a staple meal in our home (without the chillies for the kids). Not only is it super easy, quick and delicious, but it is also loaded with good carbs, proteins and fats.

SERVES: 4 • PREP TIME: 25 min • COOKING TIME: 20 min • LEVEL OF DIFFICULTY: 3/5

INGREDIENTS

2 Tbsp sesame oil

3 Tbsp Thai green curry paste

2 cm piece fresh ginger, grated

3 spring onions, finely chopped

1 long red chilli, deseeded and finely chopped
  (optional)

2 Tbsp tamari

1 tsp coconut sugar

10–12 florets tenderstem broccoli
  (or 1 small head broccoli)

1⅔ cups light coconut milk

⅔ cup snow peas

¼ cup roughly chopped fresh coriander

¼ cup Thai basil (if you can't find, use regular basil)

1 pack Fry's Vegan Chicken-style Strips or 300 g
  plant-based chicken or 1 block firm tofu, pressed to
  remove water and then cubed

1 tsp sesame oil

2 Tbsp maple syrup

2 Tbsp sesame seeds

METHOD

In a large pan heat the sesame oil over a medium-high heat. Add the curry paste, ginger, spring onions and chilli, then sauté for approximately 2 minutes or until fragrant. Add the tamari, coconut sugar, broccoli, coconut milk and peas. Bring to a simmer over a low heat and cook for 10–12 minutes. Add the coriander and basil in the last 5 minutes of cooking and stir through thoroughly.

In a separate pan, lightly fry the vegan strips or tofu in the sesame oil until warmed through (approximately 6 minutes). Add the maple syrup and allow to caramelise over the strips or tofu (approximately 2 minutes). Remove from the heat and sprinkle over the sesame seeds.

Serve with basmati or jasmine rice.

MASSAMAN THAI CURRY

1 SERVING

1   1   1

Slightly sweeter than the traditional Thai curries, with the inclusion of some of my favourite spices (cardamom, cinnamon, cloves and nutmeg) this Thai curry traces its roots back to a Persian influence. The spices in massaman paste are also all loaded with antioxidants.

SERVES: 4 • PREP TIME: 10 min • COOKING TIME: 10 min • LEVEL OF DIFFICULTY: 2/5

INGREDIENTS

2 Tbsp sesame oil

300 g firm tofu, pressed and cut into 2 cm cubes

½ tsp ground turmeric

½ tsp ground cinnamon

3 Tbsp soy sauce

1 red pepper, sliced into 1 cm strips

1 cup fresh green beans, halved

½ medium head cauliflower (200–250 g), broken into florets

3 spring onions, thinly sliced

2 cm piece fresh ginger, grated or finely sliced

3 Tbsp massaman curry paste (store bought, but check the ingredients as some curry pastes contain fish)

1¾ cups light coconut milk

2 Tbsp peanut butter

1 Tbsp maple syrup

1 head bok choy (90–100 g), roughly chopped

Garnish

1 long red chilli, deseeded and chopped

chopped fresh coriander to taste (optional)

black sesame seeds

1 spring onion, finely sliced

METHOD

In a large frying pan, heat 1 tablespoon of the sesame oil over a medium-high heat. Fry the cubed tofu along with the turmeric and cinnamon for 2–3 minutes until it starts to become golden and slightly crisp. Add the soy sauce and fry for a further 2 minutes. Remove the tofu and set aside.

Heat the remaining sesame oil in the same pan and add the pepper, green beans, cauliflower, spring onions and ginger, and fry for another 2 minutes. Still over a medium heat, add the curry paste and a three-quarter cup of the coconut milk. Stir well to ensure the vegetables are all coated with the mixture. Add the remaining coconut milk, as well as the peanut butter and maple syrup. Bring to a simmer and cook for 3 minutes. If the mixture is too thick, stir in a little water. Add the bok choy and fried tofu, then simmer for an additional 2 minutes.

Serve with rice and garnish with the chilli, coriander (if using), sesame seeds and spring onions.

ROASTED BUTTERNUT AND LENTIL LASAGNE

1 1 1 1 1

1 SERVING

Comfort food at its finest! This dish is perfect for so many occasions – cosy nights in, 'get well' or 'congrats on your new home' gifts, or having friends or family over for dinner. I usually make it over a weekend, cover will foil and bake when needed. It will keep for up to 4 days in the fridge before cooking.

SERVES: 6 • PREP TIME: 45 min • COOKING TIME: 1 hour 20 min • LEVEL OF DIFFICULTY: 4/5

INGREDIENTS

10–15 large lasagne sheets
  (store bought)
¾ cup basil pesto (see recipe
  on page 183)
vegan parmesan (see recipe
  on page 155)
sprigs fresh basil and parsley

Roasted butternut
1 medium butternut (450–550 g)
2 Tbsp extra virgin olive oil

Lentil and tomato sauce
1 Tbsp extra virgin olive oil
1 medium brown onion, finely
  chopped
1 x 400 g can brown lentils
1 cup water, room temperature
2 x 400 g cans chopped tomatoes
1 medium carrot, grated
1 baby marrow, grated
1 Tbsp tomato paste
6 brown mushrooms, sliced
¼ cup sundried tomatoes, drained

½ tsp dried rosemary
½ tsp dried thyme
½ tsp dried sage
1 tsp balsamic vinegar
1 tsp pink Himalayan salt
1 tsp coconut sugar
½ tsp baking powder

METHOD

Begin by preparing the roasted butternut. Preheat the oven to 180 °C. Peel the butternut and halve it lengthways. Remove the seeds and then slice very thinly (approximately 5 mm). Brush the slices with the olive oil, arrange on a baking tray and roast for 20–30 minutes, or until cooked through.

While the butternut is roasting, make the lentil and tomato sauce. Heat the olive oil in a large frying pan over a medium heat. Add the onion and cook for approximately 5 minutes until translucent. Add the remaining sauce ingredients and bring to a simmer, stirring often, for 25 minutes until the mixture thickens and reduces.

To assemble, layer the lasagne in a baking dish as follows: lasagne sheets and sauce; lasagne sheets, butternut slices and basil pesto. Repeat and continue in this fashion but ending with a layer of sauce. Cover with foil and bake for 30 minutes at 180 °C. Remove the foil and bake for another 10 minutes to caramelise the top. Sprinkle with vegan parmesan.

Serve the lasagne garnished with fresh basil and parsley, and a side salad.

PLANTS ON FIRE

CHICKEN-STYLE SKEWERS
WITH PEANUT SATAY

2 SKEWERS

1   1

Too good not to share. The 'chicken' in this dish may be replaced with tempeh. Keep in mind the time required for marinating, for the most delicious result.

SERVES: 4 • PREP TIME: 15 min (and 1 hour to marinate) • COOKING TIME: 10 min • LEVEL OF DIFFICULTY: 2/5

INGREDIENTS

1 x 380 g box plant-based chicken-style strips
  (e.g. Fry's) or 350 g tempeh
4–6 wooden skewers, soaked in water overnight
  (to prevent burning)

Peanut satay sauce
1 tsp coconut oil
½ brown onion, finely minced
¼ tsp crushed garlic
½ tsp grated fresh ginger
½ tsp ground cumin

4 Tbsp smooth peanut butter
2 Tbsp soy sauce
2 Tbsp tamari
1 tsp lime juice
2 Tbsp maple syrup
plant-based milk or water as needed

Toppings
thinly sliced spring onions
crushed peanuts
fresh coriander

METHOD

Defrost the chicken-style strips or cut the tempeh into medium-sized cubes (± 2 x 2 cm).

For the peanut satay sauce, heat the coconut oil in a small saucepan over a medium-high heat. Add the onion and fry for 5 minutes, then add the garlic, ginger and cumin. Fry for another 1–2 minutes. Add the peanut butter, soy sauce, tamari, lime juice and maple syrup. Lower the heat and simmer for another minute or so, until the peanut butter melts. Add a little plant-based milk or water to thin out the mixture as needed, and allow to cool.

Combine the strips or tempeh and sauce in a dish, ensuring that all are covered with the sauce. For the best results, marinate for an hour (or overnight) in the refrigerator. Thread the strips or tempeh onto the soaked skewers. Barbecue over a medium heat for 6–8 minutes a side, or alternatively cook in an oven or air fryer at 180°C for 5–6 minutes. Sprinkle the skewers with spring onions, crushed peanuts and coriander.

Serve with the remaining sauce on the side.

This is seriously addictive! Sprinkle these crispy, umami-flavoured, toasted coconut flakes on salads, potato salad or vegan omelette.

NOT-SO-TRADITIONAL POTATO SALAD
WITH COCONUT BACON

1 SERVING

2   1

A must-have with any barbecue or festive lunch is a potato salad, but often this means mayo, egg and ham. Here is my plant-based version without mayo, egg or ham.

SERVES: 4–6 • PREP TIME: 15 min • COOKING TIME: 12 min • LEVEL OF DIFFICULTY: 2/5

INGREDIENTS

1 kg whole baby potatoes, scrubbed

6 heaped Tbsp vegan mayo

1 Tbsp fresh lemon juice

1 tsp coconut sugar

½ tsp smoky ground paprika

1 Tbsp Dijon mustard (wholegrain works best)

1 red onion, finely diced

½ stalk celery, finely sliced

salt and pepper to taste

½ cup coconut bacon (see below)

a small bunch fresh flat-leaf parsley, finely chopped

METHOD

Place the baby potatoes in a large pot and cover with cold water. Bring to the boil and simmer for 10–12 minutes until tender. Drain and allow to cool slightly. Halve the potatoes and place them in a large bowl.

Whilst the potatoes are boiling, combine the vegan mayo, lemon juice, coconut sugar, paprika, mustard, onion and celery in a bowl, and mix well. Season to taste. Gently stir the mayo mixture into the warm potatoes until they are well coated. Sprinkle over the coconut bacon and parsley leaves.

COCONUT BACON

PREP TIME: 20 min

INGREDIENTS

2 cups coconut flakes

1 tsp coconut oil

1 tsp smoky paprika

1 Tbsp maple syrup

2 Tbsp tamari

1 Tbsp liquid aminos (optional)

METHOD:

Preheat the oven to 180°C and line a baking tray with baking paper. Combine all the ingredients, then spread on the baking tray in an even layer. Bake for 15 minutes but keep checking as coconut can overcook and burn very easily. The coconut should be dry and slightly browned. Leave to cool before storing in an airtight container in the freezer. Use as required.

SUPER EASY, FOOL-PROOF
BEER BREAD

1 SLICE

The name says it all. When unexpected guests arrive and you need a hot loaf of bread to go with your dinner or barbecue, this is your go-to recipe! Trust me.

MAKES: 1 loaf • PREP TIME: 5 min
• COOKING TIME: 45 min • LEVEL OF DIFFICULTY: 1/5

INGREDIENTS

500 g self-raising flour
   or gluten-free flour
   with 2 tsp baking
   powder and 1 tsp
   xantham gum

1 x 330 ml beer,
   preferably ale
1 tsp fine Himalayan salt
1 Tbsp extra virgin
   olive oil

METHOD

Preheat the oven to 180°C. Grease a loaf pan (12 x 18 cm) with cooking spray or coconut oil. Combine the flour, beer and salt to form a loose dough and all the flour is just incorporated. Do not overmix. Add the mixture to the bread pan and bake for 45–50 minutes, or until the bread sounds hollow when you tap the top. Remove from the oven and drizzle with a splash of olive oil and ground salt. Serve immediately.

VARIATIONS

Garlic and herb: Add 1 teaspoon of mixed dried herbs and ½ teaspoon of garlic powder to the bread mixture.
Middle Eastern spice: Toast ½ teaspoon cumin seeds and add them to the bread mixture along with ¼ teaspoon ground coriander, ¼ teaspoon ground cinnamon and ¼ teaspoon onion powder.

RED CABBAGE STEAKS

1 STEAK

1   1

Low calorie main or best veggie side dish — whatever you decide — these 'steaks' are crunchy-juicy-umami taste-sensations.

SERVES: 6–8 • PREP TIME: 5 min
• COOKING TIME: 35 min • LEVEL OF DIFFICULTY: 3/5

INGREDIENTS

1 red cabbage (850–950 g)
2 Tbsp sesame oil
3 Tbsp white miso paste
6 Tbsp teriyaki sauce
(store bought or see
recipe on page 85)

¼ cup sunflower seeds
salt and pepper to taste
1 Tbsp sesame seeds

METHOD

Preheat the oven to 180°C and line a large baking tray with foil. Cut the cabbage lengthways into 15 mm-thick 'steaks'. The core of the cabbage should hold the 'steaks' together. Place on the prepared baking tray and brush both sides of each 'steak' with the oil. Bake for 35 minutes or until the 'steaks' start to char slightly.

Meanwhile, in a small bowl mix the miso paste and teriyaki sauce. Keep a basting brush handy. Remove the 'steaks' from the oven (but do not switch off the oven) and brush each with a mixture of paste and sauce. Season with salt and pepper, if necessary, and sprinkle with the seeds. Place in the oven for another 5 minutes. Serve hot.

VEGGIE SLIDER PATTIES – 3 WAYS

1 SERVING= 2 BURGERS

Prepare the base recipe and then make 3 variations that are guaranteed to delight even the pickiest eater. Choose from a spicy sweet potato and coriander, a sweet beetroot and caramelised onion or an umami shiitake, sesame and miso version, or make them all.

SERVES: 6 • PREP TIME: 30 min • COOKING TIME: 10 min
• LEVEL OF DIFFICULTY: 2/5 • MAKES: 12 patties (4 from each variation)

INGREDIENTS

Base mixture

1 x 400 g can mixed beans,
  rinsed and patted dry
1 x 400 g can chickpeas, rinsed
  and patted dry

Spicy sweet potato and
  coriander patties

1 medium sweet potato
⅓ base mixture
1 Tbsp tomato paste
2 Tbsp panko crumbs
½ tsp salt
¼ tsp black pepper
1 tsp dried oregano
½ tsp ground paprika
¼ tsp cayenne pepper
juice of ¼ lemon
a handful of fresh coriander,
  finely chopped

2 Tbsp all-purpose flour
1 Tbsp olive oil

Sweet beetroot and caramelised
  onion patties

1 tsp coconut oil
½ brown onion, finely chopped
1 Tbsp coconut sugar
⅓ base mixture
2 baby beetroots, cooked
  (store bought is fine to
  save time) and finely chopped
2 Tbsp panko crumbs
1 tsp dried thyme
¼ tsp ground ginger
½ tsp ground coriander
½ tsp fine salt
¼ tsp freshly ground black pepper
¼ tsp ground cinnamon
1 Tbsp balsamic vinegar
juice of ¼ lemon

2 Tbsp all-purpose flour
  (plus extra if required)
1 Tbsp olive oil

Shiitake, sesame and miso patties

⅓ base mixture
½ brown onion, chopped
8 shiitake mushrooms,
  finely chopped
2 Tbsp panko crumbs
1 Tbsp miso paste
1 tsp sliced spring onion
¼ tsp crushed garlic
½ tsp fine salt
½ tsp freshly ground black pepper
1 Tbsp sweet soy sauce
½ tsp ponzu (optional)
2 Tbsp all-purpose flour
  (plus extra if required)
1 Tbsp white and black sesame seeds
1 Tbsp extra virgin olive oil

METHOD

For the **base mixture**, pulse the beans and chickpeas in the bowl of a food processor, but keep some of the chunkiness of the beans. Divide into thirds and set aside.

For the the **spicy sweet potato and coriander patties**, peel the sweet potato, cut into cubes and steam for 15 minutes until soft, then mash. Combine the base mixture, mashed sweet potato, tomato paste, panko, salt, pepper, oregano, paprika, cayenne pepper and lemon juice. Add the coriander. Using your hands, roughly shape the patties, using the flour to prevent the mixture from sticking to your hands. Heat the olive oil in a non-stick pan and fry the patties for 5–6 minutes, turning often to prevent them from burning. Alternatively, place the patties on a medium-heat grill and brush with the olive oil. Grill for 7–8 minutes, turning regularly.

For the **sweet beetroot and caramelised onion patties**, melt the coconut oil over a medium-high heat, then sauté the onion for 3–4 minutes. Add the coconut sugar and cook until the onions start to brown. Remove from the heat and allow to cool. In a bowl, combine the base mixture with the caramelised onion, chopped beetroot and all the remaining ingredients, except the olive oil. This mixture will be slightly wet, so add flour as required. Using your hands, roughly shape the patties, using the extra flour to prevent the mixture from sticking to your hands. Pour the olive oil into a non-stick pan and fry the patties for 5–6 minutes, turning often to prevent burning. Alternatively, place the patties on a medium-heat grill and brush with olive oil. Grill for 7–8 minutes, turning regularly.

For the **shiitake, sesame and miso patties**, combine the base mixture, brown onion, mushrooms, panko, miso paste, spring onion, garlic, salt, pepper, soy sauce, ponzu (if using) and flour. Mix well. Using your hands, roughly shape the patties, using the flour to prevent the mixture from sticking to your hands. Lightly roll each patty in the sesame seeds. Pour the olive oil into a non-stick pan and fry the patties for 5–6 minutes, turning often to prevent burning. Alternatively, place the patties on a medium-heat grill and brush with olive oil. Grill for 7–8 minutes, turning regularly.

Shiitake, sesame and
miso patties

NOTE: Freeze in an airtight
container for up to 3 months.

Spicy sweet potato
and coriander
patties

Sweet beetroot
and caramelised
onion patties

LOADED HOTDOGS
WITH SALSA, CRISPY ONION RINGS AND CURRIED MUSTARD

1 HOT DOG

1   1   1

Saturdays were made for these bad boys. This is #veganfood at its finest, so save it for Saturdays or barbecues with friends, or picnics in the park, or whenever 'sometimes food' is needed.

SERVES: 8 • PREP TIME: 45 min • COOKING TIME: 20 min • LEVEL OF DIFFICULTY: 2/5

INGREDIENTS

8 plant-based hot dog sausages
  (e.g. Fry's)
8 hot dog rolls
vegan cheese (optional)

Curried mustard sauce
⅓ cup Dijon mustard
1 spring onion, finely sliced
1 tsp curry powder

¼ cup almond milk
a pinch of sugar

Onion rings
1 onion, sliced into rings
sunflower oil, for deep frying
½ cup all-purpose flour
½ cup cornflour
¼ cup polenta
½ tsp salt

½ cup almond milk
¼ cup coconut cream

Salsa
½ cucumber, finely chopped
1–2 avocadoes, chopped
½ red onion, finely chopped
1 Tbsp fresh lemon juice
2 tsp olive oil
salt and pepper to taste

METHOD

For the curried mustard sauce, combine all the ingredients in a small saucepan over a medium heat and simmer for 2 minutes. Blend with a hand blender or in a food processor until smooth and set aside to cool.

For the onion rings, separate the onion slices into rings. Heat the sunflower oil over a medium-high heat until it reaches 180°C. (Test this before frying by placing one ring in the oil. If it bubbles immediately, the oil is ready.) Stir all the dry ingredients together in a large mixing bowl. Combine the almond milk and coconut cream in a separate mixing bowl. Dip each onion ring into the dry mixture, then dip into the wet mixture and then back into the dry mixture. Fry the rings in batches until golden and crisp (1–2 minutes). Drain on a paper towel and set aside.

For the salsa, combine all the ingredients in a bowl.

Lightly chargrill the hot dog sausages on a barbecue grid over medium-hot coals until heated all the way through. Slice each roll, lengthways, without cutting all the way through. Spread the roll with the curried mustard sauce, then add the hot dog sausages and top with salsa and onion rings. Add some vegan cheese for an extra treat.

COCONUT-CHILLI-LIME STRIP KEBABS

WITH TOASTED COCONUT AND FRESH LIME

2 KEBABS

1   2

SERVES: 4 • PREP TIME: 30 min • COOKING TIME: 10 min • LEVEL OF DIFFICULTY: 1/5

INGREDIENTS

8 wooden skewers, soaked in cold water overnight
  or soaked in boiling water for 15 minutes
1 x 380 g box chicken-style strips (e.g. Fry's),
  slightly defrosted
1 red pepper, sliced into thick strips
1 red onion, sliced into thick strips

Coconut-chilli lime marinade
100 ml soy sauce
150 ml coconut milk

juice of 2 limes, reserve a little for serving
¼ cup apple cider vinegar
¼ cup maple syrup
3 cloves garlic, crushed
1 tsp grated fresh ginger
1 red chilli, deseeded and roughly chopped
salt and freshly ground black pepper to taste

To serve
½ cup toasted coconut flakes
½ tsp dried chilli flakes (optional)

METHOD

For the marinade, place all the ingredients into the bowl of a food processor and blitz until combined. Set aside.

Thread the chicken-style strips onto the wooden skewers, alternating with slices of red pepper and red onion. Pour over the marinade and leave to marinate for 15–20 minutes (or overnight if possible).

Heat the braai to a medium-high heat and grill for 5–8 minutes, turning often. Remove from the heat and immediately sprinkle with the lime juice that was set aside.

To serve, sprinkle the coconut and chilli flakes over the kebabs.

SLOPPY JOES

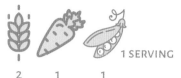

2   1   1   1 SERVING

Anything with the name Sloppy Joe is worth making, right? Popularised in the 1930s, inexpensive cuts of meat were extended with tomato and onion, and served with bread as a type of sandwich. Genius! So here is my reinvented, vegan-friendly version!

SERVES: 8 • PREPARATION TIME: 15 min
• COOKING TIME: 30 min • LEVEL OF DIFFICULTY: 2/5

delish

INGREDIENTS

1 Tbsp extra virgin olive oil

1 medium brown onion, finely chopped

2 cloves garlic, crushed

2 tsp ground cumin

2 tsp smoky paprika

1 tsp ground coriander

2 Tbsp tomato paste

1 green pepper, diced

1½ cups plant-based mince (e.g. Fry's)

1 long red chilli, deseeded and finely chopped (optional)

1 Tbsp brown sugar

1 x 400 g can chopped tomatoes

½ cup halved rosa or baby tomatoes

1 Tbsp balsamic vinegar

2 tsp soy sauce

2 tsp hoisin sauce

1 cup vegetable stock (see recipe for vegetable stock paste on page 140)

1 x 400 g can lentils, rinsed and drained

salt and pepper to taste

8 hamburger rolls, sliced in half

1 red onion, finely chopped

a handful of fresh coriander, finely chopped

a handful of micro herbs to garnish

METHOD

Heat the oil in a saucepan over a medium heat. Add the onion and garlic and sauté for 2 minutes. Stir in the cumin, paprika and ground coriander and fry for another minute, taking care not to burn the spices. Add the tomato paste and green pepper and sauté for 2 minutes to caramelise the tomato paste slightly.

Add the mince and fry for 2 minutes then stir in the chilli, sugar, canned and fresh tomatoes, balsamic vinegar, soy and hoisin sauce and stock. Simmer for 12–15 minutes, uncovered, over a low heat until thickened. Stir in the lentils and simmer for 3–5 minutes. Season to taste.

To assemble the Sloppy Joes, spoon some of the mince mixture onto the bottom half of each roll. Add a sprinkling of chopped onion, fresh coriander and micro herbs. Cover with the top half of the rolls and serve.

BATCH COOKS

BATCH COOKS 101

Could batch cooks be the new fairy godmother of food preparation? With all the pressures of life, meal preparation can not only be intimidating, but also seem impossible. Parents are trying to juggle so many balls at once, and there is never enough time in the day to think about healthy family meals. Not to mention the absolute lack of creativity at 6pm with a few hungry mouths to feed. I totally get it!

Batch cooking has transformed the way I feed my family and gives me a few precious minutes extra in the evenings to play a game with my kids or help them with their homework.

WHAT IS BATCH COOKING?

Batch cooking is the pre-preparing of recipes, which can be mixed and matched to create a variety of meals throughout the week. These meals are what I refer to as 'bases', and which will work with various other 'last-minute-quick-cooks' such as rice, quinoa or salads. For me, batch cooks are usually done on a Sunday and typically take around 1½ hours to prepare. It's also a good time to do your juicing for the week, prepare overnight oats, chia breakfast bowls or even just wash and cut veggies for use later in the week.

WHY IS BATCH COOKING SO ON TREND?

* Getting into the habit of batch cooking will save time during the week and alleviate mealtime stress, creating more time to help kids with homework, empty the dishwasher, take washing off the line, put your feet up, meditate or go for a quick walk.
* One mess, one clean. Enough said!
* You'll eat more whole plant-based foods – no more last minute, highly processed foods or take-out, which will result in a healthier, happier you!
* You'll save money. Buying your food in bulk and preparing it at home is much cheaper than buying ready meals and takeout.
* Workplace lunches will be transformed. Leftovers and batch cooks are lifesavers when it comes to packing lunch – no more junk food from the canteen.
* You will feel like a rock star – being organised and having everything in place when you get home from work gives you such a sense of achievement – this alone, makes batch cooking worthwhile!

STEPS TO CREATE A BATCH COOK PLAN

1. Plan your meals for the week or have an idea of the meals you think you may like. Some examples:
   - ☐ Chilli can be served with roasted sweet potato, or eaten with tacos and guacamole. You can roll it into a wrap to make a burrito, or even spooned onto a slice of sourdough.
   - ☐ Red lentil dal can be served alongside a quick curry, or packed for school in a flask with toasted wraps, or eaten with sliced avocado for breakfast.

☐ Bolognese sauce can be used to make a lasagne, served with pasta, or eaten with sourdough bread.

☐ Roasted sweet potatoes can be added to a Buddha bowl or salad jar, thrown into a curry, or stirred through a leafy, green salad.

☐ Pre-cut veggies are great to serve with hummus, added to lunchboxes, or eaten as a snack throughout the day.

☐ Vegan granola makes a great breakfast, lunchbox snack, or pre-workout snack.

2. Try to cook at least 2 bases, 2–3 veggies (just wash and chop or pre-cook too) and 2 legumes (chickpeas, black beans). I make a lunchbox option for the kids as well, such as bliss balls, granola bars or muffins.

3. Make a shopping list. Don't shop when you are hungry and be disciplined about keeping to the list. The pantry chapter (see page 38) has a comprehensive list of foods, herbs and spices to have on hand. It's a helpful starter list, which you can build on as you gain experience. Another way to maintain shopping discipline is to order fruit and veg from a local organic produce company and have them delivered on a Friday or whenever convenient for your chosen batch cook day.

4. Clear your diary to accommodate batch cook day, turn on some music and get cooking.

RED PEPPER AND BLACK BEAN CHILLI

1   1   1   1 SERVING = 1 CUP

Thank goodness for Mexico, because I swear life would not be the same in my house without this recipe! Chilli is one of the most versatile batch cooks – think chilli on toast, ladled over baked potatoes, served with corn chips, in toasted wraps, or even served with rice. It can be eaten after school instead of sugary snacks, or even packed for school or work in a small flask.

SERVES: 6–8 • **PREP TIME:** 10 min • **COOKING TIME** 35 min • **LEVEL OF DIFFICULTY:** 2/5

INGREDIENTS

2 Tbsp extra virgin olive oil

2 red or brown onions, diced

2 yellow, orange or red bell peppers, diced

2 cloves garlic, crushed

2 stalks celery, sliced

2 tsp chipotle spice

1 Tbsp chopped fresh or dried oregano

2 Tbsp ground cumin

1 tsp ground cinnamon

1 Tbsp ground smoky paprika

2 Tbsp red wine vinegar

2 tsp coconut sugar

2½ cups vegetable stock (2½ Tbsp of vegetable stock paste, see page 140)

2 x 400 g cans chopped tomatoes

4 x 400 g cans beans (mixture of black beans and kidney beans)

1 x 400 g can whole kernel corn or 2 whole corn on the cob (mealies)

1 tsp freshly ground black pepper

salt to taste

METHOD

In a large, heavy-based pot, heat the olive oil over a medium-high heat. Add the onions, peppers, garlic and celery and sauté for 6–8 minutes. Add the chipotle spice, oregano, cumin, cinnamon and paprika, then sauté for another 2 minutes, taking care not to burn the spices. Add the vinegar and sugar. Cook for a few seconds until the vinegar has evaporated.

Pour in the stock and canned tomatoes. Stirring often, cook uncovered over a low heat for 20 minutes. Add all the canned beans, corn and pepper, and cook for a further 5 minutes over a medium heat. If using corn on the cob, boil for 15 minutes and char on a hot griller pan before slicing off the kernels.

Season to taste. Garnish as desired and serve with fresh guacamole, toasted wraps or corn chips.

COCONUT RED LENTIL DAL

1 SERVING   WITH COCONUT CREAM

1   1   1

A staple in my Sunday #batchcooks, this dal doesn't usually make it past Tuesday … it's that good!

SERVES: 6–8 • PREP TIME: 10 min • COOKING TIME: 30 min • LEVEL OF DIFFICULTY: 1/5

INGREDIENTS

2 Tbsp coconut oil

2 brown onions, finely diced

2 cm piece fresh ginger, grated

2 cloves garlic, crushed

1 long red chilli, deseeded and finely chopped

1 Tbsp garam masala

2 tsp ground coriander

1 tsp ground cumin

1 x 400 g can crushed tomatoes

2 stalks celery, finely sliced, OR 2 grated
    baby marrows

2 carrots, grated

1 cup coconut cream or coconut milk

1 cup water

1½ cups vegetable stock (use 1½ Tbsp vegetable
    stock paste, see recipe on page 140)

2 cups dried split red lentils, rinsed

To serve

coconut yoghurt and fresh coriander

METHOD

In a large pot, heat the coconut oil over a medium-high heat. Add the onions and sauté for 5 minutes. Add the ginger, garlic, chilli, garam masala, ground coriander and cumin, then sauté over a low heat for another 2 minutes. Take care not to burn the spices and add a little water if necessary. Add the tomatoes, celery or baby marrows, carrots, coconut cream or milk, water and vegetable stock. Simmer, uncovered, for 15–20 minutes, stirring occasionally. Add the rinsed lentils and cook for a further 10 minutes, stirring occasionally, until the lentils are tender.

    Serve with a dollop of coconut yoghurt and a sprinkling of fresh coriander.

DAL MAKHANI

1 1 1

1 SERVING = 1 CUP

Dal makhani hails from Punjab in northern India. It is possibly the most popular dish served in Indian restaurants and homes and there's no doubt in my mind why this is the case. I could eat it every day, it's that delicious! Although it's traditionally made with heaps of butter or ghee, I have created a lower fat, vegan version that I think you and your family will love!

SERVES: 6–8 • PREP TIME: 10 min • COOKING TIME: 35 min + plus soaking time • LEVEL OF DIFFICULTY: 2/5

INGREDIENTS

1½ cups dried black lentils

4½ cups water

2 Tbsp coconut oil

2 cinnamon sticks (± 3 cm each)

2 tsp cumin seeds

2 dried bay leaves

1½ heaped Tbsp garam masala
  or curry powder

1 tsp ground turmeric

2 tsp ground coriander

½ tsp ground smoky paprika

1 brown onion, diced

2 cm piece fresh ginger, minced

3 cloves garlic, crushed

1 x 400 g can crushed tomatoes

1 tsp brown sugar

1 tsp fine salt

½ tsp cayenne pepper

½ x 200 ml can coconut cream

1½ cups water

salt to taste

To serve

fresh coriander

long red chillies, chopped

cooked basmati rice

METHOD

Soak the lentils for more than 6 hours, preferably overnight. Rinse them under cold, running water 3 or 4 times before cooking. In a large pot, bring the lentils and 4 cups of water to a simmer for 25–35 minutes until tender.

Meanwhile, place the coconut oil in a heavy-based saucepan over a medium heat. Add the cinnamon sticks, cumin seeds and bay leaves. Stir the spices and cook until fragrant (about 3 minutes), being careful not to burn them. Add the garam masala or curry powder, turmeric, ground coriander and paprika, and cook for 2–3 minutes while stirring. Add the onion, ginger and garlic and continue cooking for 3 minutes. Place the canned tomatoes into the bowl of a food processor and purée until smooth. Add the puréed tomatoes, sugar, salt and cayenne pepper to the spiced onion and garlic mixture, and simmer for 5 minutes.

By now, the lentils should be cooked. Drain them and add to the tomato and spice mixture. Pour in the coconut cream and 1 cup of water, and cook for 15 minutes. You can adjust the thickness by adding more liquid or cooking uncovered to evaporate some of the liquid. Season to taste.

Serve with fresh coriander, chopped chillies and basmati rice.

'Only when the last tree has been cut down, the last fish caught and
the last stream poisoned will we realise we cannot eat money'

CREE INDIAN PROPHECY

SPLIT PEA DAL WITH PICKLED RED ONION

1 SERVING

1 1 1

Another one of my all-time favs, split pea dal is filled with nutritious ingredients, and antioxidant-filled spices. It's delicious as a dal or a soup. Bring on winter.

SERVES: 6 • PREP TIME: 10 min • COOKING TIME: 30 min • LEVEL OF DIFFICULTY: 1/5

INGREDIENTS

250 g green split peas, soaked in cold
    water overnight
2 Tbsp coconut oil
1 medium brown onion, chopped
2 cloves garlic, crushed
2 cm piece fresh ginger, grated
2 tsp garam masala
1 tsp ground coriander
1 Tbsp ground cumin
1 Tbsp ground turmeric
½ tsp freshly ground black pepper
1 long red chilli, deseeded and chopped (optional)
2 carrots, grated
2 cups coconut milk

1½ cups hot vegetable stock (use 1½ Tbsp vegetable
    stock paste, see recipe on page 140)

Pickled red onion
1 red onion, thinly sliced
juice of ½ lime
lime zest to taste
½ tsp salt
½ tsp sugar

To serve
pickled red onion, chopped fresh coriander, toasted
    coconut, a squeeze of lemon

METHOD

Rinse the split peas thoroughly until the water runs clear. Drain well and set aside.

In a heavy-bottomed pot, heat the coconut oil over a medium-high heat. Sauté the onion, garlic and ginger for 4–5 minutes until the onion is translucent. Add the spices and chopped chilli. Sauté over a low heat for 1–2 minutes until fragrant. Add the carrots, coconut milk and vegetable stock, then bring to a simmer. Add the split peas and cook over a medium heat for 25 minutes, stirring often to avoid burning.

To make the pickled red onion, combine all the ingredients and allow to stand for a few minutes, before serving. It can be stored in an airtight container in the fridge for a few days.

Serve the dal with the pickled red onion, chopped coriander or toasted coconut and a squeeze of lemon.

HOMEMADE VEGETABLE STOCK PASTE

This stock can be refrigerated for up to 3 months.

MAKES: 200 ml–1 cup • PREP TIME: 10 min
• COOKING TIME: 40 min • LEVEL OF DIFFICULTY: 1/5

INGREDIENTS

4 stalks celery, roughly
   chopped
3 carrots, roughly chopped
1 baby marrow, roughly
   chopped
1 tomato, roughly
   chopped
1 large onion, roughly
   chopped
1 clove garlic, chopped
150 g Himalayan salt
3 tsp olive oil

Herbs (as many as possible)
1 fresh bay leaf
1 bunch fresh flat-leaf
   parsley, chopped
a handful of fresh sage,
   chopped
a handful of fresh basil,
   chopped
1 sprig fresh rosemary,
   leaves only

METHOD

Add all the ingredients to a blender or food processor and blend to a very fine-textured paste. Place in a heavy-bottomed pan and cook over a low heat for 20 minutes stirring continuously to prevent burning. Once cooked, place back in the blender or food processor and blend until smooth. Place a sterilised jar in an ice bath and quickly transfer the paste to the jar. Once cool, refrigerate immediately.

NOTE: For recipes in this book, 1 heaped tablespoon of the paste mixed in 1 cup boiling water will make 1 cup of stock.

HOMEMADE TOMATO SAUCE

For those last-minute Friday dinners, spread the sauce over a premade pizza base or wrap, load with veggies and vegan cheese and dinner is done. This sauce will win over the fussiest of eaters. Double up on the ingredients if making as a pasta sauce for 4 people.

MAKES: 2 cups • PREP TIME: 5 min
• COOKING TIME (if cooked): 15 min
• LEVEL OF DIFFICULTY: 2/5

INGREDIENTS

1 x 400 g can chopped
    tomato or 350 ml
    passata
6 Tbsp sundried
    tomatoes in oil
1 Tbsp coconut sugar
1 Tbsp vegan miso paste
    or 1 Tbsp coconut
    aminos (optional)

2 cloves garlic, crushed
6 fresh basil leaves,
    roughly chopped
1 tsp dried oregano
½ tsp fine salt
¼ tsp freshly ground
    black pepper

METHOD

To prepare a no-cook pizza sauce, place all the ingredients in the jug of a blender and blend until smooth. That's it! If you prefer to cook the sauce, blend all the ingredients until smooth, then transfer the mixture to a heavy-based saucepan. Cook over a medium heat, stirring often, for 10–15 minutes. If the sauce starts to burn add a tablespoon of water. Store in a sterilised airtight container in the fridge for up to 4 days.

MEXICAN CHILLI NON CARNE

1 SERVING = 1 CUP

1   1   1

A delicious, flavoursome and filling base for tacos, burritos and nachos, or simply serve with rice or a side salad. This chilli non-carne can be made in a matter of minutes or in advance for an easy mid-week meal!

SERVES: 6 • PREP TIME: 5 min • COOKING TIME: 20 min • LEVEL OF DIFFICULTY: 2/5

INGREDIENTS

2 Tbsp extra virgin olive oil

1 red onion, finely chopped

1 clove garlic, crushed

1 long red chilli, deseeded and finely chopped
    (optional)

1 x 300 g pack plant-based mince,
    defrosted (e.g. Fry's)

12–14 portobello mushrooms, finely diced

½ cup walnuts, roughly chopped

1 Tbsp finely chopped chives

2 Tbsp tomato paste

1 tsp ground smoky paprika

¼ tsp chilli powder

½ tsp garlic powder

1 tsp ground cumin

1 tsp chipotle spice

1 tsp dried oregano

1 x 400 g can organic black beans, drained and rinsed

½ x 400 g can whole kernel corn, drained

Himalayan salt to taste

METHOD

In a large saucepan, heat the olive oil over a medium-high heat. Sauté the onion, garlic and chilli in the oil until the onion is translucent (3–5 minutes). Add the mince and fry over a high heat until it starts to brown. Add the mushrooms, walnuts, chives, tomato paste, spices and oregano and fry for a further 5 minutes. Reduce the heat to low and add the drained beans and corn. Leave to cook, stirring occasionally, for 5 minutes. Season to taste.

   Serve with fresh guacamole (page 77), vegan sour cream (page 98) and tacos!

LENTIL BOLOGNESE

1 SERVING = 1 CUP

1   1

For those last-minute pasta nights or precooked dinners, this recipe is simple, quick to make and nutritious, with a good amount of protein, thanks to the lentils! Another great batch cook to alleviate mid-week meal-prep stress!

SERVES: 4–6 • PREP TIME: 20 min • COOKING TIME: 35 min • LEVEL OF DIFFICULTY: 2/5

INGREDIENTS

2 Tbsp extra virgin olive oil

1 medium brown onion, chopped

½ cup sundried tomatoes in oil, drained

2 cups sliced brown mushrooms

3 cloves garlic, crushed

2 x 400 g cans chopped tomatoes

1 tsp brown sugar or coconut sugar

½ tsp Himalayan salt

1½ Tbsp dried oregano

10 fresh basil leaves

2 x 400 g cans brown lentils,
   drained and rinsed

¾ cup pitted kalamata olives (optional)

3–4 Tbsp red wine (optional)

METHOD

Heat 1 tablespoon of the olive oil in a large saucepan over a medium-high heat. Add the onion and sauté for 5 minutes. Add the drained sundried tomatoes, mushrooms and garlic and fry for another 3–4 minutes over a medium-high heat. Add the chopped tomatoes, sugar, salt, herbs, lentils, olives and red wine (if using). Simmer over a low heat for 15 minutes or until the lentils are tender and the sauce is reduced. If the sauce becomes too dry during the simmering, add a few tablespoons of water and stir through.

Serve with your favourite pasta.

GIGANTES PLAKI
(GIANT BAKED BEANS)

1 SERVING = 1 CUP

1   1

If the Mediterranean diet is touted to be the best diet to achieve longevity and two of the Blue Zones are in Greece, then the Greeks may be onto something. This dish is not only deliciously satisfying, it is also loaded with wholesome ingredients.

SERVES: 6–8 • PREP TIME: 10 min • COOKING TIME: 2 hours • LEVEL OF DIFFICULTY: 1/5

INGREDIENTS

2 Tbsp olive oil

2 medium brown onions, chopped

3 cloves garlic, minced

4 Tbsp tomato paste

2 x 400 g cans chopped tomatoes

2 tsp coconut sugar

2 tsp dried oregano

2 tsp fresh thyme, or 3 tsp dried thyme

1 tsp ground cinnamon

1 tsp freshly ground black pepper

1 tsp Himalayan salt

1 cup vegetable stock (made with 1 heaped Tbsp vegetable stock paste, see recipe on page 140)

3 x 400 g cans butter beans, drained and rinsed

a handful of chopped fresh parsley, to garnish

METHOD

Preheat the oven to 140°C. In a large frying pan, heat the olive oil over a medium heat. Lightly sauté the chopped onions and garlic for 2–3 minutes until fragrant. Add the tomato paste, chopped tomatoes, coconut sugar, oregano, thyme, cinnamon, pepper and salt. Stir well until all the ingredients are well combined. Remove from the heat, then add the stock and beans, and stir through. Transfer the mixture into an uncovered casserole dish and place in the oven for 2 hours.

Garnish with fresh parsley and serve with crusty sourdough bread.

NOTE: I have made this dish in 1 hour at 200°C. It isn't quite as flavourful but hits the spot if you are in a hurry. I recommend batch cooking the dish and storing in the fridge for up to 1 week. It becomes tastier with time.

If you prefer using dried lima beans, soak the beans overnight, drain and then boil in a few cups of water for 2 hours first. Rinse and then add to the tomato sauce, before placing in the oven.

LOVE YOUR GUT

'All dis-ease begins in the gut'

Hippocrates

Perhaps the most non-engineered part of the human body is the gut membrane. It measures somewhere between 40 m² and 300 m² (depending on the scientist doing the measuring), but even at 40 m², that is an enormous area, which essentially performs the task of filtering toxins and waste from the body and allowing nutrients through.

Managing gut health is of major importance, because gut function and health of the gut biome are linked to overall health and wellbeing, and even moods.

THE MICROBIOME

Your body hosts trillions of microorganisms; in fact 99% of our physical make up is actually bacteria. The highest and densest microbe population can be found in the gut, where they play a critical role in digestion, weight regulation, and immune system function. We are only as healthy as our gut bacteria. Our modern lifestyle, the foods we consume, and our overuse of antibiotics has changed the gut biome and has partly been responsible for disease epidemics, such as autism, Alzheimer's, food intolerances, cancer, depression and anxiety, to name only a few. The new emerging science and study of the gut is extremely exciting as we may just be discovering the key to good health and wellness.

SO HOW DO YOU BUILD A HEALTHY GUT BACTERIUM?

Remember that everyone is an individual and our needs are different, but these broad guidelines will help you to develop a healthy gut biome.

1. Eat a wide variety of plant-based foods. The diversity of whole plant foods is a crucial first step. Count the number of different plant foods you eat in a day and start to build on that number.
2. Increase your fibre intake. Fibre feeds the healthy bacteria which, in turn, improve immune function, reduce inflammation and chronic disease, and even help regulate mood. By eating more plant-based foods you will naturally boost fibre intake.

3. Only eat organic or spray-free produce. The pesticides sprayed onto crops are in part responsible for breaking the tight junctions that hold together the cells that make up the gut lining. This damage to the gut results in an overreaction by the immune system every time we consume food. The permeations or holes in the gut allow for toxins to leak through into the bloodstream resulting in an overreaction from the immune system and an inflammatory response. Normally the macrophage will clear the offending toxin, but with leaky gut, the immune system can be overwhelmed* (refer to diagram alongside).

*www.ncbi.nlm.nih.gov/pmc/articles/PMC3945755/

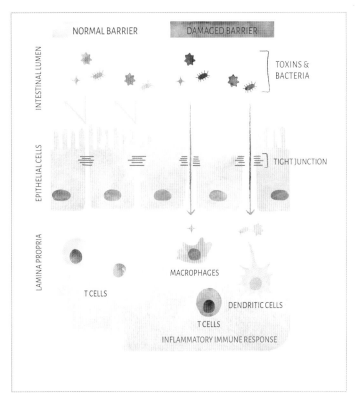

4. Ensure you add a prebiotic to your diet. These are easy to obtain from the food you eat, but it may be easier to use a prebiotic supplement. Prebiotics support the growth of the good bacteria in the gut. They are a precursor to probiotics and are so often overlooked when it comes to gut health.
5. Probiotics are the live microorganisms or healthy bacteria. Fermented foods are a great way to get a healthy dose of probiotics. Live cultures found in coconut yoghurts, kefir, kimchi, sauerkraut and kombucha will all build a good gut biome.
6. If you take antibiotics, make sure you boost your pre- and probiotics afterwards.
7. Spend time in nature and breathe in the air from these natural environments. The bacteria in the air will build your gut biome – so get down to the beach, go walking in the forest and climb a mountain. Your gut will thank you.
8. A holistic view on gut health is important too, so make sure you follow the 8 keys to good health (see page 22).

Note to mums: If you find your child craves sugar, displays poor behaviour patterns and mood swings, develops various food intolerances or is generally unwell and catching every bug going around, you may need to work on improving their gut biome. Follow the same guidelines as above.

Where possible, breastfeed your baby. Your milk contains a wide variety of bacteria that help build a 'good' biome.

A QUICK GUIDE
TO FERMENTING AT HOME

Fermenting foods to preserve them goes back thousands of years, before fridges, freezers or chemical preservatives. Sauerkraut (fermented cabbage), soy sauce (fermented soy beans), pickled vegetables, wine (fermented grapes) and kombucha (fermented tea) are all examples of fermented foods. Unfortunately, Western society has forgotten the art of fermentation as modern food science has progressed.

Our current systems of sterilisation, pasteurisation, chemically preserving and radiating foods destroys bacteria. Without distinguishing between good and bad, they destroy the good bacteria too.

TYPES OF FERMENTATION

Lacto-fermentation: a process of fermentation whereby starches and sugars are broken down into lactic acid. It enhances the nutritional benefits of the food by improving the bioavailability of the minerals in the food as well as producing beneficial gut bacteria. We use lacto-fermentation to make sauerkraut, kimchi and sourdough.

Alcohol fermentation: where yeasts break down starches or sugars into alcohol and carbon dioxide molecules. This fermentation is used to make wine and beer.

Acetic acid fermentation: where starches and sugars from fruit ferment into vinegar. This type of fermentation is used to make apple cider vinegar or kombucha. For this to occur, a living culture needs to be added, for example a SCOBY or 'mother' or yeast. A SCOBY is an acronym for 'symbiotic culture of bacteria and yeast'.

TIPS FOR SUCCESSFUL FERMENTING

1. Establish 'starter' cultures. This may be in the form of a SCOBY or liquid from a previous ferment. You may need a good probiotic supplement. These starter cultures will help start the new fermentation process. Ask a friend to donate a SCOBY or order one online. It should be light in colour. A dark SCOBY usually means it is old.
2. Keep everything clean and always use filtered water. Bad bacteria will grow where the good bacteria grow, so you need to ensure that all your utensils, jars and surfaces are sterilised before starting.
3. Storing a ferment correctly is critical. Use a thoroughly cleaned glass jar with a lid. You will need to release air from the ferment as gas is produced and the jar could explode. To start the fermentation process, a warmer temperature is best, so don't place it in the fridge. Cool air will slow down the ferment. Heating a ferment can also destroy microbes – don't cook fermented foods.
4. Use fresh ingredients for your ferment – the fresher the better.
5. Don't ferment whole vegetables – always cut or grate the vegetables as this allows water to be drawn out.
6. Add salt to the vegetables. This promotes the movement of liquid out of the vegetable and encourages the growth of the good bacteria over the bad bacteria.
7. Compress the vegetables and ensure that they are fully submerged in their own brine. This will cause the bad bacteria to die off completely and preserve the food.
8. Play with other ingredients – add different spices or vegetables to your ferments to create new flavours.

COCONUT YOGHURT

1 SERVING = ¼ CUP

1

PREP TIME: 5 min • FERMENTATION TIME: 2 days

INGREDIENTS

4 probiotic capsules or
coconut yoghurt starter
2 x 400 ml cans coconut milk
(additive free and full-fat) or
4 cups homemade coconut milk
(see page 156)

METHOD

In a sterilised jar, stir the probiotics into the coconut milk. Cover the jar with a cloth and secure with an elastic band. Leave the jar on your kitchen counter for 2 days, before refrigerating. Eat within 5 days.

Serve with a drizzle of maple syrup, homemade granola and fresh berries.

INGREDIENTS/UTENSILS

3.5 litres water

1 cup sugar

8 teabags (green, Rooibos or black)

5 litre glass jar

1 cup starter liquid
  (from your last brew)

1 SCOBY

tea towel and rubber band

berries, ginger, apple, cinnamon,
  lime (all optional) (to be added to
  the second fermentation)

METHOD Boil 2 litres of water in a saucepan. Remove from the heat and stir in the sugar until it dissolves. Add the tea bags and allow to stand for 5 minutes. Once the tea has cooled to room temperature, remove the tea bags, transfer to a jar and add another 1.5 litres of room temperature water to the jar.

Add the starter liquid (this creates an acidic environment that prevents harmful bacteria from growing and multiplying). Add the SCOBY. Secure the tea towel over the mouth of the jar with an elastic band. Remember the kombucha needs to breathe. Place the kombucha in a dark place where the temperature is 20–25°C. Never place in the fridge as this slows down the fermentation process.

Whilst the tea is fermenting, you may see the SCOBY moving around the jar, or you may notice another SCOBY growing, or there may be small strands floating around. These are all normal, so don't throw it out.

Start tasting the brew after 7 days – if you find the tea to be too sweet, continue brewing for longer. When it tastes too much like vinegar, it has brewed for too long. Once you are happy with the taste, bottle the kombucha into smaller bottles with lids. You may want to strain the kombucha as you are pouring it, to remove any 'floating bits'. Leave at least 2 cups of liquid in the jar – this will be the starter tea for your next batch.

Leave the bottled kombucha in a dark area at room temperature for another 3 days. This will carbonate it, which gives it a fizziness (children love all things fizzy, so don't leave out this step). This is the stage to add optional ingredients. You can strain these out before drinking. Store the bottles in the fridge and drink within 30 days. Start your next batch.

SAUERKRAUT

¼ CUP

1

MAKES: 1 medium jar • PREP TIME: 5 min • FERMENTATION TIME: 3 weeks • LEVEL OF DIFFICULTY: 1/5

INGREDIENTS

1 medium cabbage (purple or white and ideally organic)

2 Tbsp fine Himalayan salt (not table salt or iodised salt)

beetroot, carrots, lemon zest, ginger or garlic (all optional, but should not make up more than 20% of the kraut)

1 sterilised jar

METHOD Remove the outer leaves of the cabbage and reserve. Cut the cabbage in half and remove the core, then thinly slice the cabbage. Add the cabbage and salt to a bowl and toss with your hands. Add any of the optional ingredients. Place handfuls of the mixture into the jar and press down as you go to compact the cabbage and remove any air. The liquid created in the process should just cover the cabbage – if not, add a little water to ensure all the cabbage is covered. Fold the reserved outer cabbage leaves over the top of the kraut mixture to create a 'lid'. Use the cabbage core or a carrot to create a wedge between the lid and the folded cabbage leaves. This will keep the pressure on the cabbage so that it remains submerged.

The sauerkraut will be ready to eat after a few days, ideally, at around 3 weeks. You can keep the kraut months after you made it as long as it smells fine or there are no signs of mould growth.

FERMENTED CASHEW CHEESE

2 TBSP
1

MAKES: 1 round
• PREP TIME: 10 min, 1 day prep, 2 days ferment
• LEVEL OF DIFFICULTY: 2/5

INGREDIENTS

200 g raw cashew nuts
2 tsp nutritional yeast
2 Tbsp lemon juice
a pinch of lemon zest
   (optional)
1 clove garlic, minced
1 tsp fine Himalayan salt
pepper to taste

2 Tbsp sauerkraut juice
   (or the powder from
   1 probiotic capsule)
finely chopped dill,
   cracked black pepper
   or smoky paprika
   for serving

METHOD

Place the nuts in a jar. Pour over enough water to cover the nuts and soak for a few hours. Rinse and drain the nuts. Place the nuts, yeast, lemon juice, zest, garlic, salt and pepper in a blender and blend until smooth. Add the sauerkraut juice or probiotic powder and blend for an additional 10 seconds. Transfer the mixture to a cheesecloth over a colander. Fold the cheesecloth over the mixture and secure with an elastic band. Leave on the kitchen counter for approximately 48 hours to allow fermentation to occur (which will bring out the flavours).

Form the cheese into a disc shape and place in the fridge to chill for a few hours before serving. Serve with dill, black pepper or paprika.

DAIRY ALTERNATIVES

VEGAN PARMESAN

1 SERVING = 1 TBSP

½

MAKES: 1½ cups • PREP TIME: 5 min
• LEVEL OF DIFFICULTY: 1/5

INGREDIENTS

¾ cup raw cashew nuts

¼ cup nutritional yeast

¼ tsp garlic powder

¼ tsp onion powder

½ tsp fine Himalayan salt or to taste

METHOD

Place all the ingredients into a blender and blend until the mixture resembles a fine crumb. Taste, and add more salt if needed.

Store the mixture in an airtight container in the fridge for up to 3 months.

VEGAN RICOTTA

1 SERVING = ¼ CUP

1

MAKES: 1 medium jar (± 2 cups)
• PREP TIME: 5 min • LEVEL OF DIFFICULTY: 2/5

INGREDIENTS

1 cup blanched raw almonds

1 cup raw cashews nuts

1 cup unsweetened almond milk

salt and pepper to taste

METHOD

Soak the almonds and cashews overnight.

Drain and rinse the nuts, then add them to a high-speed blender with the almond milk, salt and pepper. Blend until smooth and creamy.

Store in an airtight container in the fridge for up to 1 week.

RICE MILK

½ 1 CUP

Think 'pink milk' or chocolate milk … be creative. Add cacao for chocolate, or strawberries for pink or even, blue seaweed powder for blue and see how long it lasts in the fridge. My kids love this homemade, healthy version of flavoured and coloured milks. Pack it in their lunchboxes or keep it chilled for an after-school treat.

MAKES: 1 litre • PREP TIME: 5 min + overnight soak
• LEVEL OF DIFFICULTY: 1/5

INGREDIENTS

1 cup uncooked white rice
4 cups filtered water
1–2 Tbsp maple syrup
½ tsp vanilla essence

METHOD

Soak the rice overnight in water. Drain the rice and add the filtered water. Stir in the maple syrup and vanilla essence. Blend in a powerful blender until smooth. Strain the milk through a nut milk bag into a jug. If you don't have a nut milk bag, a T-shirt works too! Seal the jug and store in the fridge for up to 5 days.

COCONUT MILK

½ 1 CUP

Coconut milk is probably my favourite milk for making fruit smoothies and bowls. This recipe is super-simple and makes a delicious coconut milk in a few minutes.

MAKES: 1.5 litres • PREP TIME: 5 min
• COOLING TIME: 1 hour • LEVEL OF DIFFICULTY: 2/5

INGREDIENTS

2 cups shredded unsweetened coconut
4 cups hot water (just below boiling)

METHOD

Place coconut and water in a blender. Use caution as some blenders that are completely sealed may explode from the pressure build-up caused by hot water. I use a blender with an opening at the top to release steam. Blend for 3 minutes on high speed until creamy. Strain through a strainer first to remove any larger coconut pieces and then strain through a nut milk bag or cheesecloth. Bottle and refrigerate. Coconut milk may be stored in the fridge for 3–4 days.

'Milk coconuts,
not cows'

ALMOND NUT MILK

½ 1 CUP

MAKES: ±1 litre • PREP TIME: Overnight soaking + 5 min
• LEVEL OF DIFFICULTY: 1/5

INGREDIENTS

1 cup raw almonds
1 litre filtered water
a pinch of salt

METHOD

Soak the almonds overnight in a jar of water. Drain the nuts, then add them to a processor, along with the filtered water and salt. Blitz until a smooth, milk-like consistency is reached. Strain through a nut milk bag. Bottle and store in the fridge for up to 5 days.

CASHEW NUT MILK

½ 1 CUP

And you thought making your own milk would be tough. This is about as easy as it gets. And drinking homemade milk ... well, let's just say, heaven.

MAKES: ±1 litre • PREP TIME: Overnight soaking + 5 min
• LEVEL OF DIFFICULTY: 1/5

INGREDIENTS

200 g cashew nuts
1 litre filtered water
2 tsp rice malt syrup (optional)
½ tsp ground cinnamon (optional)
a pinch of salt

METHOD

Soak the cashews overnight in a jar of water, then drain. Add the nuts, filtered water, rice malt syrup, cinnamon (if using) and salt to a blender and blend until a smooth, milk-like consistency is reached. Bottle and keep in the fridge for up to 5 days. If you'd prefer a very smooth milk, strain through a nut milk bag.

Chocolate Truffles →

Scrumptious Caramel
Choc-Nut Bars

Seed and Amaranth
Snack Bars →

Cinnamon and
Walnut Muffins

Oat and Choc →
Cookies

TREATS

FOOD ON THE GO
AND LUNCHBOXES

Being prepared is the best way to avoid reaching for those last-minute, expensive, empty-calorie snacks when the hunger bug bites! Some of the recipes in this book are perfect for snacking, lunchbox options or desk meals (although I do not for one minute recommend eating while working!).

HERE ARE SOME IDEAS

Overnight oats (page 60)

Edamame beans

Celery boats

Edible red pepper fruit bowls

Popcorn

Good-fat-keto-nola (page 62)

Vietnamese rice paper rolls (page 74)

Raw veggies

Raw nuts/nut butter

Corn tortillas (page 80)

'Sushi' jars (page 84)

Breakfast balls (page 166)

Seed and amaranth snack bars (page 174)

Toasted chickpeas

Veggie slider patties (page 118)

Cashew fried rice (page 97)

Chocolate truffles (page 175)

Leftovers

PREPARING A HEALTHY AND YUMMY LUNCHBOX

Perhaps the most stressful part of each morning is packing the all-important lunchbox. It's not only creatively challenging (to avoid boredom too), but a minefield that requires some careful navigation.

This is what goes through my head on a typical school morning while packing the boy's lunchboxes. (Humour me if you don't have children!)

☐ What do they actually like to eat?

☐ What don't they like? (and it's different for each child)

☐ And even if they like it, could it include an allergen that may affect others in the class?

☐ What is healthy? How much sugar, protein, fats and carbs are they getting? Have I met all the needs of a perfectly nutritionally balanced lunchbox?

☐ What do I have in my pantry/fridge? (I am in trouble if I don't have fruit, because a lunchbox should always contain fruit, or at least that's the expectation).

☐ Do I have anything other than apples?

☐ Does the lunchbox look exciting?

☐ Does it all look homemade?

☐ How much single-use plastic is inside the lunchbox?

☐ I wonder if the teacher may be paying attention and judging me for the packet of popcorn?

☐ Will a friend have a much more enticing lunchbox?

☐ How many other kids get tuck shop money?

☐ How many times can a child eat Vegemite or Marmite on a sandwich?

☐ Is there something in the lunchbox that could be considered a treat? (We all want a surprised and happy child.)

☐ Does the lunchbox need an ice pack?

☐ Will the whole lunchbox come back untouched, because they didn't want to miss out on playtime?

☐ Am I a good parent?

You get my point. This lunchbox thing is tough.

HERE ARE SOME TIPS FOR MAKING LUNCHBOXES AN EASIER AND ALMOST-STRESS-FREE EXPERIENCE.

If you pack wholesome, nutrient-dense foods into a lunchbox, you can reduce the volume of food. For example: cashew fried rice (packed into a thermo-flask) will leave them feeling fuller for longer, whereas a packet of crisps or chocolate bar will give them an energy surge, but leave them feeling hungry and tired just a short while later.

Make sure there is a good source of carbohydrates in the lunchbox – wholegrains are best.

Protein is easy to add to the lunchbox – think plant-based nuggets, peanut butter or nuts, edamame beans, toasted chickpeas, protein balls or hummus

Add whole fruits rather than fruit juice. Whole fruits contain fibre, which slows down the metabolism of sugar and will leave a child (or yourself) feeling fuller for longer.

Choose snack bars that are low in sugar or make your own. Breakfast balls are a great snack option too and can be used to hide a variety of superfoods like goji berries, amaranth, hemp seeds, chia seeds, cinnamon, moringa powder or daily greens.

Make sure you pack a bottle of water – if your child doesn't like water, add a slice of orange or mint leaves to the water and a few blocks of ice on a hot day.

Make sure you have a Bento-style lunchbox or a variety of smaller, reusable containers. This makes packing with less single-use packaging easier.

Get your kids involved and give them some choice. When they are involved, they will start learning so much about nutrition and what good, healthy foods are.

BANANA LOAF

1   1   1   OR   1   1 SLICE

A huge passion of mine is sourcing alternative ingredients for popular foods, to make them healthier. I remember my Gran's banana bread, which was incredible, so the thought of banana bread always conjures up good memories. Now you can recreate this old favourite with gluten-free, refined sugar-free and vegan ingredients.

MAKES: 1 standard loaf • PREP TIME: 15 min • COOKING TIME: 30 min • LEVEL OF DIFFICULTY: 2/5

INGREDIENTS

3 very ripe, medium bananas, mashed

½ cup desiccated coconut

2 tsp ground cinnamon

½ cup rice malt syrup or maple syrup

1 tsp vanilla paste

80 g coconut butter or margarine, melted

2 flax eggs (2 Tbsp ground flaxseed mixed
    with ¼ cup water)

2 cups all-purpose flour (or gluten-free flour mix)

2 tsp baking powder

⅓ cup chopped walnuts

METHOD

Preheat the oven to 180°C and grease a standard loaf pan with cooking spray or melted coconut oil. In a mixing bowl, combine the mashed bananas, coconut, cinnamon, rice malt syrup and vanilla paste. Mix in the coconut butter or margarine and the flax eggs. Add the flour and baking powder and mix until the flour is just incorporated; do not overmix. Gently fold in the walnuts, then transfer the mixture into the prepared loaf pan and bake for 30 minutes. A skewer inserted into the loaf should come out clean. Leave to cool before slicing.

OAT AND CHOC COOKIES

1 COOKIE

1

This is one of those cookies that your grandkids will be asking you for the recipe one day.

MAKES: 15 • PREP TIME: 10 min
• COOKING TIME: 12 min • LEVEL OF DIFFICULTY: 2/5

INGREDIENTS

1½ cups rolled oats
½ cup almond flour
1 cup all-purpose flour
1 tsp baking powder
¼ tsp fine salt
140 g vegan butter or
  margarine
150 g coconut sugar
2 flax eggs (2 Tbsp
  ground flaxseed mixed
  with 6 Tbsp water and
  set aside for 5 minutes)
70–80 g vegan chocolate
  chips

METHOD

Preheat the oven to 160°C and line a large baking tray with baking paper. Blitz the oats in a food processor for a fine textured oat flour. In a medium-sized bowl, combine the oat flour, almond flour, all-purpose flour, baking powder and salt. In another large bowl, beat the butter or margarine and sugar until white and creamy (3–4 minutes). Add the flax eggs and beat until combined. Add the dry mixture to the wet mixture and mix until there are no lumps. Add the chocolate chips and stir until well distributed.

Using your hands, shape 15 golf-sized balls (the dough should be slightly sticky – not too wet and not too dry). Place them on the prepared baking tray and flatten each with your hand or a spoon. Bake for 12–15 minutes. Leave to cool on an wire rack and store in an airtight container.

COCONUT GINGER COOKIES

1 COOKIE

1

I have a soft spot for cookies, and my favourites are ginger cookies. I think this slight addiction started when I was in my first trimester. Luckily, my kids love ginger too and we get to bake and enjoy these gluten- and refined sugar-free ones together.

MAKES: 15–20 cookies • **PREP TIME:** 10 min
• **COOKING TIME:** 10 min • **LEVEL OF DIFFICULTY:** 2/5

INGREDIENTS

1 cup raw cashew nuts	½ tsp baking soda
½ cup crystallised ginger	(bicarbonate of soda)
½ cup rolled oats	½ tsp ground cloves
1 cup desiccated coconut	½ tsp ground cinnamon
⅓ cup maple syrup	1 tsp ground ginger
3 Tbsp coconut oil	½ tsp ground cardamom
	1 tsp vanilla bean paste

METHOD

Preheat the oven to 180°C and line a baking tray with baking paper. Place the cashew nuts and ginger in a food processor and blitz until fine. Add the rest of the ingredients and continue to process until the mixture comes together. Roll handfuls of cookie dough into small balls. Place on a lined baking tray, leaving space for cookies to spread, and press down slightly using the palm of your hand or a fork.

Bake for 10 minutes until browned at the edges. Allow to cool before storing in a container.

BREAKFAST BALLS

| 1 | ½ | 1 | 2 BALLS |

Or any time balls, really! You will need a powerful food processor and ideally a few kids on your production line. They are excellent at rolling and decorating them with desiccated coconut.

MAKES: ± 20 balls • PREP TIME: 10 min
• LEVEL OF DIFFICULTY: 1/5

INGREDIENTS

2 cups organic rolled gluten-free oats
½ cup activated raw almonds
½ cup desiccated coconut, plus extra ¼ cup
½ cup chia seeds
½ cup goji berries
½ cup almond or macadamia nut butter
1 Tbsp ground cinnamon

½ cup LSA (linseed/ flaxseed/ground almonds) or make your own by mixing 150 ml flaxseed, 100 ml sunflower seeds and 50 ml ground almonds
1 Tbsp cacao powder
¼ cup melted coconut oil
1 cup pitted dates
¼ cup rice malt syrup or maple syrup

METHOD

Add all the ingredients to a food processor, except the extra ¼ cup of coconut. Blend until the mixture comes together (feel it with your fingers). If it's too dry, you may need to add a little more coconut oil. Once the mixture starts holding together, start rolling into bite-sized balls and dipping into the extra coconut. Store the breakfast balls in the fridge and enjoy them anytime. They will keep for about a week, but it's unlikely that they'll last longer than 1 or 2 days!

CHAMOMILE-GINGER-LEMON ENERGY BARS

1 BAR

1

Where three is better than one.

MAKES: 8–10 bars • PREP TIME: 20 min
• LEVEL OF DIFFICULTY: 2/5

INGREDIENTS

½ cup cashew nuts
½ cup walnuts
1 cup pitted dates
¼ cup chopped dried
  apples
¼ cup dried apricots
2 Tbsp hemp seeds
1 Tbsp dried chamomile
  (from chamomile
  tea bags)

1 Tbsp freshly grated
  ginger
1 tsp vanilla paste or
  a few drops vanilla
  essence
juice of ½ lemon

METHOD

Place the nuts and dried fruit into a food processor and blend until the mixture is roughly chopped and starts holding together. Add the remaining ingredients and blend until completely mixed. Shape into small bars by placing the mixture between two sheets of baking paper, rolling out to the desired thickness and then cutting into rectangles or squares.

Store in an airtight container in the refrigerator.

SCRUMPTIOUS CARAMEL CHOC-NUT BARS

1 SQUARE

1

MAKES: 15 bars • PREP TIME: 20 min • FREEZING TIME: 1 hour (or longer)
• COOLING TIME: 20 min • LEVEL OF DIFFICULTY: 4/5

INGREDIENTS

Bars

¾ cup dry-roasted almonds

⅔ cup rice malt syrup

1 Tbsp soy milk

¼ cup melted coconut butter

1 tsp Himalayan salt

1 tsp vanilla paste

1 cup chunky peanut butter

Chocolate coating

140 g dark vegan chocolate

1 Tbsp coconut butter

METHOD

Pour the almonds into a paper bag and roll with a rolling pin to crush. It's up to you how chunky a texture you prefer. Heat the rice malt syrup in a pan until it starts bubbling. Allow it to bubble for 3 minutes. Add the soy milk and bring back to the boil for another 3 minutes. Add the melted coconut butter, salt, vanilla paste and peanut butter, then stir over a low heat until all the ingredients have blended together and turned into a smooth paste. Stir through the crushed almonds.

Line a baking tray with non-stick baking paper. Pour the peanut butter mixture onto the baking paper and fold the paper over to hold the peanut butter mixture in place. The mixture should be approximately 1 cm deep. Place in the freezer for a minimum of 1 hour.

For the chocolate coating, use a double boiler or place a glass bowl over a pot of simmering water (the water shouldn't touch the bowl). Add the chocolate and coconut butter to the bowl and keep stirring until the mixture melts and is completely smooth.

Cut the frozen peanut butter mixture into bars. Lift all the bars from the baking paper – they may be slightly sticky so peel them off with a spatula – and dip the bars, one by one, into the melted chocolate.

Place the bars on a cooling rack (place some baking paper or paper towel under the cooling rack to catch the dripping chocolate).

Once all the bars have been coated, place the cooling rack in the fridge for 20 minutes for the coating to set. Store the bars in an airtight container in the fridge for up to 2 weeks.

CINNAMON AND WALNUT MUFFINS

1 MUFFIN

1

Cinnamon not only tastes amazing when added to desserts, smoothies and savoury dishes, but it's one of nature's superfoods. This spice has powerful medicinal benefits as a potent antioxidant and anti-inflammatory. Just a quarter teaspoon a day can lower the risk of some chronic diseases. (Ok, I might be trying too hard to make muffins look like a health food!)

MAKES: 12 muffins • PREP TIME: 10 min • COOKING TIME: 16 min • LEVEL OF DIFFICULTY: 2/5

INGREDIENTS

Cinnamon streusel
¼ cup rolled oats
2 Tbsp chopped walnuts
2 Tbsp coconut flakes
¼ tsp ground cinnamon
¼ tsp ground nutmeg
1 Tbsp coconut sugar
2 Tbsp melted coconut oil

Muffins
¾ cup wholewheat spelt flour
¾ cup all-purpose flour
½ cup coconut sugar

2 tsp ground cinnamon
2 tsp baking powder
½ tsp baking soda (bicarbonate of soda)
¼ tsp fine salt
2 flax eggs (2 Tbsp ground flaxseed, stirred into
   ¼ cup water and set aside for 5 minutes)
¾ cup unsweetened almond milk
⅓ cup melted coconut oil
1 tsp vanilla essence
½ Tbsp fresh lemon juice

Optional
¼ cup raisins or dried cranberries or vegan chocolate
   (if you're feeling cheeky)

METHOD

Preheat the oven to 180°C. Line a 12-cup muffin pan with paper liners. For the streusel, combine all the ingredients in a small bowl and set aside. For a finer streusel, blitz in a food processor. For the muffins, add both flours, sugar, cinnamon, baking powder, baking soda and salt to a medium-sized bowl. Make a well in the centre.

In a separate bowl, whisk together the flax eggs, almond milk, coconut oil, vanilla essence and lemon juice until well combined. Pour into the well in the dry ingredients. Add optional ingredients. Stir the mixture just enough to moisten all the flour, but do not overmix. Divide the batter among the muffin cups and top with the streusel. Bake for 16–18 minutes or until a toothpick inserted comes out clean. Allow to cool on a rack before serving.

RASPBERRY AND ALMOND-
CACAO FUDGE

1 PIECE

1

This gluten- and refined sugar-free fudge is a perfect lunchbox snack or after-dinner treat.
The raw cacao powder will satisfy any choccy cravings.

SERVES: 8–10 • SOAKING TIME: 2–3 hours or overnight • PREP TIME: 15 min
• REFRIGERATION TIME: 4 hours • LEVEL OF DIFFICULTY: 2/5

INGREDIENTS

250 g raw almonds
250 g raw cashew nuts
½ cup coconut oil
½ cup maple syrup

125 g cacao powder
1 cup freeze-dried raspberries
   or goji berries

METHOD

Line a baking sheet (24 x 18 cm) with baking paper. Soak half the almonds and all the cashew nuts in cold water for 2–3 hours. Preheat the oven to 160°C and roast the remaining almonds for 10 minutes on the prepared baking sheet. (You can also dry-toast them in a frying pan.) Once fragrant, roughly chop the roasted almonds. Drain the soaked nuts well and place in the bowl of a food processor. Add the coconut oil and syrup and blitz until quite smooth. Add the cacao and blitz for another 30 seconds. Place the mixture into a bowl and fold through half of the chopped nuts and half of the raspberries or goji berries. Press the mixture into the same baking sheet you used to roast the almonds and sprinkle over the rest of the nuts and raspberries. Lightly press them in. Refrigerate for 4 hours to set, and then cut into triangles or squares.

SEED AND AMARANTH SNACK BARS

1 BAR

1   1

The bars are great for lunchboxes, snacks on the go or crumbled over a bowl of coconut yoghurt, and drizzled with berry compote for another snack option. Don't throw away the crumbs!

SERVES: lots of kids • PREP TIME: 10 min • COOKING TIME: 20 min • LEVEL OF DIFFICULTY: 2/5

INGREDIENTS

2 cups rolled oats
¼ cup puffed amaranth
¼ cup pepita seeds or hulled pumpkin seeds
¼ cup hulled sunflower seeds
¼ cup white sesame seeds
1 cup desiccated coconut
1 tsp vanilla essence
1 tsp ground cinnamon
½ cup melted coconut oil
½ cup rice malt syrup

METHOD

Preheat the oven to 180°C and line a baking tray (24 x 18 cm) with baking paper. Place all the ingredients in a large bowl and mix well. Press the mixture into the baking tray until it's about 1 cm thick. Bake for about 20 minutes (watch, so it doesn't burn). Remove from the oven and allow to cool slightly (10–15 minutes). Cut into bars before completely cooled as the bars harden and will become more difficult to cut. Cool completely and store in an airtight jar.

CHOCOLATE TRUFFLES

1 TRUFFLE

1

According to my son, these little chocolate balls are 'the bomb'. Just a few minutes to make and they go down a treat in lunchboxes, at school bake sales and birthday parties.

MAKES: 12 truffles • PREP TIME: 10 min
• REFRIGERATION TIME: 1–2 hours
• LEVEL OF DIFFICULTY: 2/5

INGREDIENTS

120 g pitted dates
60 g raw hazelnuts
60 g raw cashew nuts
1 Tbsp nut butter
   (your choice)

1 Tbsp melted
   coconut oil
1 Tbsp cacao powder
80 g vegan chocolate

METHOD

Line a large baking sheet with baking paper.

Place the dates, nuts, nut butter, coconut oil and cacao powder in a food processor and blend until mostly smooth. Use your hands to shape into 12 balls.

Use a double boiler or place a glass bowl over a pot of simmering water (the water shouldn't touch the bowl). Add the chocolate to the bowl and allow to melt.

Dip each ball in the melted chocolate and place on the prepared baking sheet. Place the sheet in the fridge for 1–2 hours, until the chocolate has set. Store in an airtight container in the fridge.

GLUTEN-FREE CHOCOLATE CAKE

1 SLICE

1

This versatile and delicious cake mixture can be used for cupcakes as well.
I first made it with my cousin in my kitchen and since then, its become
my go-to birthday cake, gift cake , bake sale cake, and 'lunchbox cake'.
I leave off the icing for 'lunchbox-cake'!

SERVES: 8 • PREP TIME: 10 min • COOKING TIME: ± 40 min • LEVEL OF DIFFICULTY: 3/5

INGREDIENTS

¾ cup brown rice flour

¼ cup tapioca flour

¼ cup white rice flour

¼ cup potato starch

1 tsp xanthan gum

1 cup coconut sugar or
   castor sugar

½ cup cocoa powder

1 tsp instant coffee

2 tsp baking soda
   (bicarbonate of soda)

1 tsp baking powder

½ tsp fine salt

⅓ cup melted vegan
   butter or margarine

1 Tbsp balsamic vinegar

2 tsp vanilla essence

1 flax egg (1 Tbsp ground
   flaxseed mixed with
   3 Tbsp water and set
   aside for 5 minutes)

1 cup coconut milk, at
   room temperature

Chocolate icing

150 g sweetened dark
   vegan chocolate,
   chopped

150 ml coconut cream

½ tsp ground cinnamon

METHOD

Preheat the oven to 180°C and grease 2 x 15 cm-diameter cake tins with baking spray or coconut oil. (Note: this cake does not rise very high. You could use a single deeper tin, in which case bake for about 30 minutes.) Sift all the flours, starch, xanthan gum, sugar, cocoa powder, coffee, baking soda, baking powder and salt together into a large mixing bowl. Stir with a whisk to combine evenly, then make a well in the centre.

In a separate, smaller bowl, combine the vegan butter, vinegar, vanilla essence, flax egg and coconut milk. Whisk to mix well and pour into the well of the dry ingredients. Whisk together until just combined, then pour the mixture into the prepared baking tins. Bake for 25 minutes for the cake and 18–20 minutes for cupcakes. Insert a skewer into the centre of the cake. If it comes out clean, it is ready. Remove the cake from the oven and let it cool on a wire rack before icing.

Use a double boiler for the icing, or place a glass bowl over a pot of simmering water (the water shouldn't touch the bowl). Add the chopped chocolate, coconut cream and cinnamon to the glass bowl. As the water heats, stir the mixture until melted. Pour a quarter of the mixture over one layer of the cake and top with the second layer. Pour the rest of the icing over the cake. If you made 1 layer, simply pour the mixture over the cake. Serve with coconut ice cream or vanilla coconut yoghurt.

RASPBERRY AND CHOCOLATE TARTLETS

1 TARTLET

1

These never last long, so make a double batch if you think you may need more or make more and freeze some for later. A super-simple recipe with no baking involved.

MAKES: 8 tartlets • PREP TIME: 20 min • FREEZING TIME: 3 hours • LEVEL OF DIFFICULTY: 4/5

INGREDIENTS

Base
¾ cup almond meal
   (use almond flour if you can't find meal)
10 Medjool dates, pitted
2 Tbsp cacao powder
1 tsp coconut oil

Filling
1 cup cashew nuts, soaked overnight
1 cup fresh raspberries

3 Tbsp maple syrup
1 tsp vanilla essence

Decoration
½ cup chopped dark vegan chocolate
1 Tbsp maple syrup
fresh raspberries
puffed amaranth

METHOD

For the base, place all the ingredients into a food processor and pulse to combine. Test the mixture by squeezing with your fingers; it should hold together. If not, add a little coconut oil and pulse again. Divide the mixture into 8 balls, pressing each one into a cup of a silicone muffin tray.

For the filling, add all the ingredients into a blender and combine until smooth. Pour into the chocolate bases in the muffin tray.

For the chocolate decoration, use a double boiler or place a glass bowl over a pot of simmering water (the water shouldn't touch the bowl). Add the chocolate and syrup and stir until the mixture is completely melted. Allow the mixture to cool slightly. Top the tarts with fresh raspberries and melted chocolate. Place in the freezer or fridge until set (it usually takes a few hours).

Serve sprinkled with puffed amaranth.

VANILLA NICE CREAM
WITH COOKIE CRUMBLE

    1 SERVING = 1 SCOOP   WITH CONE

1   ½   1

This one makes the nice list. Nice to eat, nice to make, nice 'n healthy too.

SERVES: 4 • PREP TIME: 5 min• LEVEL OF DIFFICULTY: 1/5

INGREDIENTS

3 frozen bananas

1 Tbsp maple syrup

a few drops natural vanilla extract

1 Tbsp cocoa powder
   (optional for making chocolate ice cream)

¼ cup coconut milk (if necessary)

crunchy oat and choc cookies (page 164)
   or any other vegan cookie, crumbled

METHOD

Add the bananas, maple syrup, vanilla extract and cocoa powder (if using) to a powerful blender and blitz until smooth. Add small amounts of the coconut milk, if required for a smoother texture.

Serve in a bowl or cones, topped with crumbled cookies or in a cone.

GIFTS MADE WITH LOVE

COFFEE AND BROWN SUGAR SCRUB

INGREDIENTS

1 cup coffee grounds

½ cup melted coconut oil

½ cup brown sugar

2 drops essential oil (e.g. cinnamon or orange) (optional)

1 drop or capsule vitamin E oil (optional)

METHOD

Mix all the ingredients in a large bowl. Decant into a jar with a sealable lid.

Remember coffee stains, so be sure to rinse off thoroughly in the shower or bath.

POST-WORKOUT EPSOM SALTS SCRUB

This one's for your workout buddies.

INGREDIENTS

1 cup Epsom salts

2 Tbsp coconut oil

2 drops any essential oil

a few dried rose petals

METHOD

Combine the ingredients until the mixture forms a coarse paste. Transfer to a jar with a sealable lid.

10-MINUTE BASIL-BROCC PESTO

1   ½   1 TBSP

MAKES: ½ cup • PREP TIME: 5 min • LEVEL OF DIFFICULTY: 1/5

INGREDIENTS

2 cups fresh basil

a handful of broccoli florets

3 Tbsp walnuts or pepita seeds

2 cloves garlic

2 Tbsp lemon juice

3 Tbsp nutritional yeast

½ tsp fine Himalayan salt

2 Tbsp olive oil

5 Tbsp water (use discretion)

METHOD

Add all the ingredients, except the olive oil and water, to a food processor and blend on high until chopped and combined. Add the olive oil a little at a time and continue to blend. Then add the water slowly until the desired consistency is reached. Store in the fridge for up to 1 week.

FESTIVE VEGAN GRANOLA

1   1

1 BOWL

SERVES: 12 • PREP TIME: 25 min • LEVEL OF DIFFICULTY: 1/5

INGREDIENTS

½ cup coconut oil

½ cup maple syrup

1–2 tsp grated orange zest

1 tsp vanilla extract

1 cup puffed amaranth

1 cup rolled oats

½ cup raw macadamia nuts

½ cup pepitas or shelled pumpkin seeds

1 tsp ground cinnamon

¼ cup dark vegan chocolate chips

½ cup dried cranberries

METHOD

Preheat the oven to 120°C and line a baking tray (25 x 35 cm) with baking paper.

In a small pot over a medium heat, melt the coconut oil until it is completely liquid. Remove from the heat and stir in the maple syrup, orange zest and vanilla.

Place all the remaining ingredients, except the chocolate and cranberries, into a bowl and mix well. Pour over the coconut oil mixture and stir until well combined and all the ingredients are coated with the oil. Spread the mixture evenly on the prepared baking tray and bake for 15–20 minutes. It can burn easily so keep checking! Once lightly browned, remove from the oven and allow to cool completely. Stir through the chocolate and cranberries once the granola is completely cool. Transfer to pretty gift jars.

SPICED CHAI TEA MIX

This lovely homemade gift will have your loved one curling up on a couch with a soft blanket, enjoying a moment that you helped create. Pop the mixture into old, unused jars and attach beautiful gift tags with the following wonderful message on the back:

Life is all about experiences, so my dear friend, curl up by a fire with a chai latte, and know in these moments that you are loved deeply, so appreciated by many and have a heart of pure gold, that nothing can stand in your way to dream and do whatever it is that makes you gloriously happy. Made With Love.

INGREDIENTS

2 cinnamon sticks, broken into smaller pieces

6 whole cloves or 1 Tbsp ground cloves

6 cardamom pods or 1 Tbsp ground cardamom

½ Tbsp ground nutmeg

3 whole star anise

1 Tbsp black tea leaves

2 tsp ground ginger

1 tsp vanilla powder or ground vanilla pod

1 tsp mushroom powder (optional) – chaga, lion's mane, reishi or cordyceps (see Note)

METHOD

Combine the ingredients in a jar, shake and store in a cool dry place.

To make a chai latte, place all the ingredients into a small saucepan, add 6 cups of water and boil for 20 minutes. Strain to remove the solids. Keep the tea in the fridge in a sealed container for up to 10 days and use as needed.

Mix half a cup of tea with half a cup of coconut or almond milk. Place in a small saucepan and bring to a boil. Add 1 teaspoon of maple syrup or sweetener.

NOTE: Different mushrooms have different functional benefits.

Chaga: supports the immune system. Take any time of the day.

Lion's mane: a powerful antioxidant, boosts the immune system and supercharges the brain.
Take in the morning or after lunch.

Reishi: its name signifies longevity and it helps to support sleep and destressing. Take it before bed.

Cordyceps: used for athletic performance and to support stamina or endurance.
Take it in the morning or pre-workout.

Chai
Tea Mix

GENERAL CONVERSIONS: METRIC TO IMPERIAL

TEASPOONS

Metric	Imperial
2 ml	¼ tsp
2.5 ml	½ tsp
5 ml	1 tsp
10 ml	2 tsp
20 ml	4 tsp

TABLESPOONS

Metric	Imperial
15 ml	1 Tbsp
30 ml	2 Tbsp
45 ml	3 Tbsp
60 ml	4 Tbsp

CUPS

Metric	Imperial
60 ml	¼ cup
80 ml	⅓ cup
125 ml	½ cup
160 ml	⅔ cup
200 ml	¾ cup
250 ml	1 cup
375 ml	1½ cups
500 ml	2 cups
750 ml	3 cups
1 litre	4 cups

RECIPE INDEX

Thank You

My name may be on the front cover of this book, but seriously,
it would not have been possible without the support and help from my tribe of special people.

Thank you to Rich, Josh and Kai – without you I don't think I would have completed this book. Having your constant understanding for me working late nights and weekends, for 'egging' me on throughout the process and eating everything I cooked or baked, even if it was my fifth attempt on one recipe in one week! And for all the hugs. I love you guys.

Thanks Dad and Mom – you guys have always been my inspiration to be better, to do better and to dream big. I have so much gratitude for being a part of the journey of getting The Fry Family Food Co. to where it is today. Let's continue to change the world, one veggie meal at a time! Love you.

Thanks to Bev – for believing in me and this book. I am forever grateful to you.

Thank you, Cecilia and Ran – my Penguin team – for bringing the book to life. You helped to capture exactly what I had envisioned, so beautifully and accurately.

Thank you, Nigel and Lisa – for making this book possible and for the many, many years we have worked together to create beautiful images that excite and inspire others to change.

Thank you, Mick – for supporting this project wholeheartedly.

Thank you to my friends and family – for inspiring so many of the recipes in this book. Every one of these recipes has a memory attached to it – our shared meals, our shared ideas and little bits of shared knowledge made this book possible. For every recipe in it was made with love.

Thank you to my Fry's team – for your constant encouragement and believing with me, that anything is possible. Thank you for being on a journey with me to make the world a better place. I am honoured to work alongside you every day.

Thank you, In the Soulshine – for the gorgeous T-shirts.

Thank you to the animal activists around the world.

Thank you to the key influencers, the vegans working within organisations creating change, the educational groups, advocacy groups, the sanctuaries and the rescue workers.

Thank you to the children who are standing up for what is right.

Thank you to the mother who delivers a delicious plant-based meal to her friend at home or sends out vegan recipes.

To the petition signers and the digital warriors, thank you.

As Margaret Mead said: 'Never doubt that a small group of thoughtful, committed citizens can change the world, indeed it is the only thing that ever has.'